UNEXPECTED PATHWAYS

The Journeys of Women in the Workforce

ANNE SOURBEER MORRIS, Ed.D.

Unexpected Pathways: The Journeys of Women in the Workforce

All rights reserved

Copyright 2015 by Anne Sourbeer Morris, Ed.D.

A. Morris Consulting, LLC acting as Futures Inspired

www.futuresinspired.com

Printed by CreateSpace

No part of this book may be reproduced or transmitted in any form or by any means, electronic or mechanical, without the written of the Publisher, except where permitted by law.

ISBN-13: 978-1505716603

ISBN-10: 1505716608

UNEXPECTED PATHWAYS

The Journeys of Women in the Workforce

Believe in the power of ya!!!
Be inspired!
Dr. Ann

Create Futures by Inspiring Futures!

—**Anne Sourbeer Morris, Ed.D.**

WITH STORIES BY:

Wynne Renee Brown, MD, Lac

Mittie Denise Cannon, Ed.D.

Bonnie Dawn Clark

Linda Eisenstein

Margie Florini

Winifred Quire Giddings

Kaitlyn Green

Mary Ann Hauser

Donna Martin Hinkle, Ed.D.

Angela Lynn Jackson Howard

Kelly Abeyta Jimenez

Latoya Rochae' Johnson

Gabrielle J. Jordan

Patricia McGlynn, Ph.D.

Christine A. Moore

Anne Sourbeer Morris, Ed.D.

Molly L. Nece

Clare Novak

Marviette Usher

Victoria N. Scott

Tina Ketchie Stearns

Dana Winner

Melissa W. Wittner

Dedication

To those who champion women …
To those who champion all!
To the *Women of Unexpected Pathways* … I thank you for
joining me on this journey!
And
To my precious daughters
Ami Morris Belcher and Jessica Anne Solesbee
To my dear grandchildren
Cadence Anne, Hunter Edward and John Michael
To those who are my family—relatives and friends alike.

May life inspire you, always!
Know that you are loved.

CONTENTS

INTRODUCTION xi
PROLOGUE—*Beginnings* xiii

JOURNEYS IN THE THIRD LIFE DECADE— THE TWENTIES

CHAPTER 1—*Can the First Years of Your Career Be the Best?* 3
    Kaitlyn Green

CHAPTER 2—*Year 1, Year 2, Year 3, Year 4 ...
I Finally Made It at 24!* 13
    Gabrielle J. Jordan

JOURNEYS IN THE FOURTH LIFE DECADE— THE THIRTIES

CHAPTER 3—*START NOW: Four Undeniable Laws
to Being What You Want to Become* 21
    Molly L. Nece

CHAPTER 4—*A Diamond in the Rough:
Everything You Need is Inside of You!* 31
    Latoya Rochae' Johnson

Journeys in the Fifth Life Decade—The Forties

Chapter 5—*A Way Paved by Curiosity* 41
    Mittie Denise Cannon, Ed.D.

Chapter 6—*Overcoming Life's Obstacles* 49
    Kelly Abeyta Jimenez *told collaboratively with*
    Anne Sourbeer Morris, Ed.D.

Chapter 7—*Caring is a Pathway* 61
    Angela Lynn Jackson Howard

Journeys in the Sixth Life Decade—The Fifties

Chapter 8—*Original Medicine* 71
    Wynne Renee Brown, MD, Lac

Chapter 9—*Paving the Road to Hell, I Found Heaven* 81
    Bonnie Dawn Clark

Chapter 10—*I AM Living the Adventure of a Lifetime, and*
So Are You ... You Just Don't Know It Yet 91
    Linda Eisenstein

Chapter 11—*Entrepreneur as Artist—*
A Winding Road Embraced 101
    Margie Florini

Chapter 12—*My Journey* 111
    Winifred Quire Giddings

Chapter 13—*Make Your Passion Your Paycheck!* 121
    Mary Ann Hauser

Chapter 14—*Life Through Pat's Eyes* 131
    Patricia McGlynn, Ph.D.

Chapter 15—*Phenomenal? What? Who Me?!* 139
    Christine A. Moore *told collaboratively with*
    Anne Sourbeer Morris, Ed.D.

Chapter 16—*Beyond Borders* 149
    Clare Novak

Chapter 17—*The Universe Will Conspire to Help You When Your Purpose is Pure!* 159
    Tina Ketchie Stearns *told collaboratively with*
    Anne Sourbeer Morris, Ed.D.

Chapter 18—*An Intentional Career and An Unexpected Life* 169
    Marviette Usher *told collaboratively with*
    Anne Sourbeer Morris, Ed.D.

Chapter 19—*Letting Go of the Parking Meter* 177
    Mclissa W. Wittner

Journeys in the Seventh Life Decade— The Sixties

Chapter 20—*Starting Again* 189
    Donna Martin Hinkle, Ed.D.

Chapter 21—*Becoming a Woman of Substance* 199
    Victoria N. Scott

Chapter 22—*Hardware, Software; Womenware* 209
    Dana Winner

Chapter 23—*The Journey to Unexpected Pathways* 221
    Anne Sourbeer Morris, Ed.D.

Epilogue—*Endings and New Beginnings* 233

Study Questions 235

Research Scaffolding Unexpected Pathways 237

About Futures Inspired 238

About The Author 239

Introduction

Celebrate your journey! Your courage, perseverance, determination or resilience will inspire! ... Your unique life journey is valued! —**Anne Sourbeer Morris, Ed.D.**

Unexpected Pathways: The Journeys of Women in the Workforce presents narratives about the career-life pathways of twenty-three women representing five life decades. The stories these women relate are stories of greatness and fragility ... stories of determination, perseverance and healing ... stories of courage, resilience and love ... stories of faith, survival and victory!

As a body of work, the volume offers generational perspective on the lives of twenty-three unique woman who share with the reader intimate thoughts about the impact of life on their career journey and vice-versa. The stories and the lessons shared are rich in inspiration. The career-life themes are undeniably connected.

The reader may view *Unexpected Pathways* as a study of these twenty-three women brought together in this volume by both design and serendipity. The volume shares the stories of individual women who embarked upon unique and personal journeys—often, quite unexpected journeys—yet the stories shared may, in part, reflect the stories of many women finding their way in life. Each story relates the intimate connection between the woman's life and her career journey. Each story and the lessons shared are written to offer hope and inspiration.

From the beginning it was our mission—*our labor of love*—to tell the stories of women's career pathways. Our goal was and is to inspire women and girls to follow their dreams. Our charge was not to recount the stories of those who were considered to be "*famous*" ... but to tell the stories of women who have quietly or sometimes not so quietly, embarked upon "unexpected" career and life journeys. There is much to be learned and pondered as the reader meets each chapter author and considers the account of her journey.

The stories in this volume are uniquely personal. It is our sincere hope that these narratives will make a difference. We hope that the spirit portrayed via these stories and the lessons shared, will inspire the reader to follow their dreams, just as each of the *Women of Unexpected Pathways*—the chapter authors—strove to follow her dream or realize her destiny. We hope that these stories offer the reader the strength to move forward with courage, hope and the understanding that there is no *right or wrong* way to live life. To move forward in the way that they and they alone envision their career-life plan—knowing that there is no right or wrong way—only their way.

> *When you are open to the possibilities ...
> who knows where life will lead?*

Be inspired!
Dr. Anne

> *Our minds may be burdened by assumption and bias, but when we look, truly look, into the hearts of others we sense the truth and may even see ourselves.* —**Anne Sourbeer Morris, Ed.D.**

Prologue

Beginnings

> *A career may create a life journey ... Life may create a career journey.* —**Anne Sourbeer Morris, Ed.D.**

In 54 BC, the Roman writer Seneca profoundly stated, *Every new beginning comes from some other beginning's end.* Our lives and our careers are in a perennial state of beginnings and endings—many quite surprising and unexpected. Despite how carefully we plan, life throws us curveballs—some we drop and some we catch victoriously. How we handle the endings and beginnings of our career-life journey makes all of the difference.

The *Women of Unexpected Pathways* are perennially growing, striving and reinventing themselves. These women have both dropped and caught the curveballs that life has thrown them. Those in the third life decade are beginning their career journey, while others seasoned with experience, may be pondering concluding journeys while also considering their next exciting project ... Life is full of possibilities—always!

Celebrate and accept who YOU are today, at this moment ... Love yourself as YOU are ... anticipate with joy the evolution to YOUR future! Great adventures lie ahead ... Be open to the possibilities!

Each chapter author, regardless of her generation, is determined to survive and to thrive in days of poverty or prosperity—success or challenge. The stories contained in this volume are a snapshot—a relative instant—in the life of each woman. I suspect, the stories will resonate with the reader who may—noting commonalities of experience or emotion—relate to the stories and to the lessons shared—gaining inspiration and strength to move forward with her or his own journey.

Frankly, the initial vision for *Unexpected Pathways* was to relate the presumably *unexpected* nature of women's career journeys, while considering the manner in which women in the workforce face barriers to their career advancement, addressing such challenges as *imposter syndrome* or *stereotype threat*—to consider the *glass ceiling*, *gender inequity* or the *wage gap*. However, as the incredible W*omen of Unexpected Pathways* shared their stories, it quickly became evident that these women were compelled to relate very personal stories—despite the initially stated vision. Many of these women, while aware of societal barriers to their career success, were fearless. Many of the women, in fact, simply ignored potential pitfalls and forged ahead following their dreams and authoring their own destinies—building their careers and their life.

The resilience, perseverance, determination and the incredible faith described by many of the chapter authors was unexpected, unsolicited and awe inspiring as the women—essentially unknown to each other in the context of this volume—related stories about their personal career journeys—some boldly and visibly embarking on their pathways and others quietly and discreetly living their lives, while greatly impacting those within their scope of influence—all making a difference. Each woman pursued her career and lived her life with conviction—her way. Please meet the *Women of Unexpected Pathways*. We begin with two women representing the third life decade—the twenties—at the beginning of their careers.

Journeys in the Third Life Decade

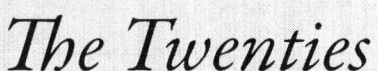

The Twenties

Chapter 1

*Can The First Years of
Your Career Be the Best?*

Kaitlyn Green

Your journey will twist and wind; it will cross mountains of success and stroll into low valleys. There will be times when you don't know which way to go—to the familiar or off to unmarked territory. The best part about the journey is that it is all yours; it is your choice to experience each step. —**Kaitlyn Green**

Blessed beyond measure, fate or in the right place at the right time ... Call my journey what you will, but through the challenges—personal and professional—my career has flourished. I love structure and strongly believe in planning and creating goals.

Foundations are crucial to the success of a child; amazing parents raised me. They gave me many gifts from their individual personalities and talent structure. I grew up with my father's entrepreneurial spirit and sales swagger; my mother's creative problem solving and organizational thinking. Growing up in a small rural town allowed me to establish lifelong relationships and value the safety of a small town. While the country element instilled in me the value of work ethic, my father's success demonstrated the value of money and allowed me to travel to different parts of the world.

As a young adult, I found my passion during large family events and the preparation that comes with them—particularly food preparation. With enthusiasm, I enrolled in a continuing education course at my high school in addition to my regular classes. Success in culinary classes and competitions grew into internships. Successful internships resulted in scholarships to Johnson and Wales University. Unexpectedly, Johnson and Wales University relocated the satellite campus that I was attending from downtown Charleston, South Carolina to the uptown area of Charlotte, North Carolina during my first year of college.

At the end of my high school career and at the conclusion of my college career, I was faced with caring for a parent with cancer—first my father and then, my mother; both during transition periods—first starting college and later, work; moving to and living in unknown cities offering new experiences and a new lifestyle. Each time, I questioned myself—should I stay at home or embark upon a new life phase? Both times, I moved forward with the love and encouragement of my parents.

Moving to the city transformed me from a well-traveled and well-spoken "country" girl to a "city" girl. This emotional and exciting transformation occurred in a short time and included my picking up multiple jobs and multiple internships. Throughout the process, I began to find my place in Charlotte. I became financially independent enough to stay through the first summer.

I learned to be a better multitasker. There were many sleepless nights as I juggled life's demands. I had a full time job as a nanny, a part time job at a church in child care, an internship with an event designer and a full class load of twenty plus hours a week. I arranged my priorities and schedules daily. I excelled academically, as I had not before in high school. I believe my academic success was due to the passion and intrigue that I experienced with my professors and course work.

I prepared for the workforce by networking at career fairs and collecting business cards from everyone in the industry that I could meet. The efforts played a major role in helping me to score my first "real" job. Of course, graduating in the year the economy hit an all-time low was a challenge. Businesses were laying-off and were hiring fewer employees let alone event planners.

At every career fair I attended in college, I collected business cards. I took time to transfer the information into an excel spreadsheet. Over the years, I built a vast industry resource. When it was time for me to find a job—after graduating and getting married—I referred to my "spreadsheet." In a down-economy, when there were no postings this resource was my only way of connecting with industry professionals and getting through the "gate keepers"—those who might block my applications. Ultimately, I interviewed for two different positions—both were sales and commission-based. I was pretty nervous about placing my livelihood on my novice ability to sell. But I was driven and young enough to accept the challenge offered to me by Clarke Allen. Clarke was a well know event designer who had planned events for Preston Bailey, David Tutera, Bob Johnson and presidents of visiting countries. I was mesmerized!

As Clarke mentored me, I learned how to sell and how to make the sales process not simply a "sell." Clarke had the gift of "selling an experience" and bringing that experience to life with a design. Many people can sell but a true sales person can sell the intangible. Aggressively, I learned the different divisions of Clarke's business and assisted him in re-branding.

The Clarke Allen Group was created in four divisions: Destination Management with local and national clients; Travel and Transportation; Set and Prop Production through Creatrix and Center Stage @ NoDa a ten-thousand square foot venue.

Under the wing of Clarke, I grew from an inexperienced planner to Senior Account Executive and an entrusted coordinator for a celebrity event designer. I managed and assisted in the management of projects with Oprah, Dr. Maya Angelou, Steve Smith and many NASCAR drivers. I worked with Siemens Energy, Coke, Dr. Pepper, NAPA, Maxim, Gentlemen's Jack, US Airways and many more. Not surprisingly, with my success came many challenges and passions.

Keeping the right emotional balance and letting go of fear were hard habits to maintain. But learn I had to. Being a planner, I wanted to control my future not just plan it. My fear of not making the cut in the event industry and the abundance of successful planners added stress. However, my fear led me to extend my motivation and effort. Juggling my desire to advance academically and keep up with the "Who's Who" in the event-world was exhausting. I also tried to pick up additional certifications and classes and go to every networking opportunity I was invited to regardless of the work load and the weekly grind. At the same time, I was uplifted when colleagues and professionals began to called me by name and see me as a peer instead of a "newbie."

Technologically speaking, my career began during a time period that evolved from the use of technology, primarily in education, to the use of technology in every aspect of working and living. Technology changed the expectation of employers, employees and clients. Technology impacted work-lifestyle balance irrevocably. My job required me to be on call 24/7 and to be accessible when needed.

In 2011, my marriage began to take a hit when my "fear" and career "drive" were consuming ninety percent of my time and energy. I was on cloud nine professionally; traveling to different parts of the country, working with celebrities and learning hands on from one of the biggest event experiential designers on the Southeastern coast. My clients and I were at a business relationship point where they only wanted to work with me and not the other seasoned account executives in the firm; all aspects of my career were top shelf.

Call it another faith opportunity. Call it what you will. Suddenly and unexpectedly, my husband was approached by an aerospace company to work for them. I actually barely remember listening as he told me about the opportunity or where the company was located, because I was too self-involved. The job offer meant that my husband's career would make great advances. The company heavily pursued Brian and made him an offer we could not refuse financially. The opportunity was critical for the advancement of his career. My husband was my foundation through my last years of school. He was my biggest supporter. I was excited for him but extremely threatened that I would lose the career I built in Charlotte.

I broke the news to my boss who was more my mentor and friend. Clarke quickly created a whole new division for me to be able to continue to work with in the company in the Triad area of North Carolina. He was so supportive not only because he knew I loved what I did but also because he knew that he would not find another event coordinator like me. Clarke had the time to teach and mold me for every aspect of selling, designing and operating The Clarke Allen Group.

I struggled to be in two places at once—with my husband in the Winston-Salem area and in Charlotte with my job. I say my job at this point because it was not my career as I quickly came to realize. My career was my passion for creating event experiences. While my position, clients and experiences would be hard to replace, the struggle personally and the exhaustion physically was overwhelming. I drove four hours a day multiple days a week to keep up with the home office and event production in our shops. During this time frame, I became pregnant with our first child but due to complications, lost the baby. The struggle to balance my career and life got harder. I woke up one morning and made a decision. Later that day, I found myself in Clarke's office explaining to him that it was time to go.

Preparing to leave The Clarke Allen Group was one of the hardest and most emotional career decisions I have made so far. In reflection, the biggest lesson that I learned was the importance of work-life balance. You must find your structure and set it in place—it will be the only way you can climb your way to success. All relationships are supposed to have two sides, not just one! This crucial lesson is still my biggest flaw. I constantly juggle and struggle with the balance of time, love and memories with my family, with the thrill and enjoyment of my career.

After relating my plans to Clarke, I continued to work on a few freelance projects for Charlotte Arrangement, the Destination Management Division of The Clarke Allen Group; while I reflected on my accomplishments and used my strengths to determine my next endeavor. I began to reach out to old hospitality connections and friends of friends in the industry.

As fate would have it, Peter Grazn, manager of The Piedmont Club, a ClubCorp property in Winston-Salem, North Carolina, learned that I was in town. Peter set up a meeting to discuss his need for reinvention of the Member Events and Private Event divisions of the club. I had worked for ClubCorp in the beginning of my career and I found it strange that I was circling back. The positions were the opposite of what I had been doing with design, transportation and destination management but were in line with my career experience with the Carolina Panthers and Venue Management of Center Stage @NoDa.

I accepted the challenge as the Private Events Director at The Piedmont Club and took over a sales plan not met in six years. I struggled with my inability to make instantaneous change and profit. This job was going to be a huge challenge. Success would require much more than just a few changes here or there. The positon required a full overhaul from venue and menu pricing to service and brand. In the past two years, I am proud to say that I have been able to grow the business twelve percent and make our sales plans with the assistance of a large renovation of the event space and experience. My success came down to determining the capacity of our events and the experiences and service *The Club* could handle, coupled with detailed marketing plans and returning satisfied members and clients.

In November 2013, my husband and I welcomed our little girl Isabella Noel. In December 2013, I faced some health concerns and was hospitalized for a week. Upon my release, with an appointment book filled with follow-up specialist appointments and a new born, I could not see how I was going to balance my career, health and new family. I began to ask myself questions like: Could I afford to be a stay at home mom? Do I want to be a stay at home mom? What is best for Isabella? In the returning weeks of my job, I asked myself the questions, Can I do my job the best? Has my career already peaked? What value besides money does my job bring to the table?

After self-reflection and a lot of support from my family, I strongly answered myself with YES! I not only can balance my growing career but I want to. The "want to" part is key; you have to love your career, I think, to satisfy your personal needs of being whole both professionally and personally. Notice I also said love your career, not your job; you will have those jobs that take you to the next level in your career that you don't particularly love. My love and passion still remains in event experiential design. I know I will find that along my career pathway in the future.

The event industry is addictive. The fast paced and ever changing "wow factors" keep me constantly enthralled. Everyone looks at their successes in different ways as achievements, blessings or benchmarks. Reflection on your accomplishments can create some of the best motivational planning for a new endeavor or self-improvement assessment. My best career decisions came from taking "another look" at where and when I started.

My hope is that my story will resonate with readers and make their journey just a bit easier or their grasp a bit greater. No path through life comes without boulders to negotiate or rivers to cross. Just remember to take advantage of your associations with dynamic and successful professionals whose wisdom and support can enrich and grow not only your professional life but your personal life as well. What wild and adventurous first years I was blessed with and I am grateful for. From my current pathway, I can clearly see now that the best is yet to come.

Kaitlyn's Five Inspired Lessons

- **Lesson #1**: Don't put anything in an email that you would not share face to face or with the person you hold in highest regard. Use social media in a positive and professional manner.
- **Lesson #2**: You can have a career and also be a GREAT Mom.
- **Lesson #3**: Build a wardrobe: They are expensive so start early.
- **Lesson #4**: Don't be afraid to speak up—Find the right time, right tone and right context.
- **Lesson #5**: Jobs are easy to find. Careers are built upon a foundation. Make sure you start with a blue print.

Dedication

To my mother, the one who instilled me with power, organization and creativeness. To my daughter who has my heart and my eyes—may the world be yours.

Kaitlyn Green, Private Events Director

The Piedmont Club—A ClubCorp Property
www.thepiedmontclub.com
Kaitlyn.green@ourclub.com

Inspiration and Introspection

Anne Sourbeer Morris, Ed.D.

Several generations ago, the mantra for many women was *we can have it all*—We can have both a family and a career! The concept at the time was revolutionary and widely criticized in some circles. Being the first women in my family to *work outside the home*, I heard both the call and the criticism loud and clear! I desperately loved my family and I loved my calling—to be an educator. I loved being a mother and a wife. I was driven to make a difference in my home and in my community.

Create your career and create your life—Your way!

Over the years, I also observed women fight for and gain significant workplace equality—to have it all—yet in many ways, the fight continues. While today, women make up fifty percent of the total workforce, equally educated, skilled women may earn only $.78 for every $1.00 a man makes for equal work.

Through her story, Kaitlyn shares her struggle with career-life balance, mirroring those of generations of women. She shares the importance of negotiation naturally built into relationships and the importance of decisions born of love. In the end, after significant self-reflection, Kaitlyn announces that she can and wants to create a healthy career-life balance. Her love of family and career motivates her to be successful personally and professionally—to be the best she can be for her family and herself. Kaitlyn is learning to take care of herself while she cares for her family and for her clients. Kaitlyn has chosen the best path for her during this moment in time ...

Unexpected Reflections

What insights or enlightenment have you, the reader, gained from Kaitlyn's chapter?

Chapter 2

Year 1, Year 2, Year 3, Year 4...
I Finally Made It at 24!

Gabrielle J. Jordan

Never give up, keep trying and working hard. Even when things are not going as planned—make a new plan, set goals and follow through. Stay focused on what is most important to YOU. Do that and you will be successful! —**Gabrielle J. Jordan**

I am a practicing engineer. I strive to promote women in engineering, letting them know engineering is not just for MEN and it is fun too! My name is Gabrielle J. Jordan. I want to take you through my *unexpected journey* that consists of my college experiences and the events following shortly thereafter. Come with me, back in time, to the tender age of 18 ...

Age 18: As a senior in high school, Princess Anne High School of Virginia Beach to be exact, I was still finalizing the details of my future; asking myself, What am I going to do for the rest of my life? I was a band *nerd* and an overall *nerd* in my all my high school classes. I made the honor roll and perfect attendance lists every year since elementary school!

My *Dad* is a <u>Mechanic</u> and my *Mom* is an <u>Engineer</u>. I always found "future" car designs and technology fascinating, so I chose to go to college to be a <u>Mechanical Engineer</u>, on a "band" scholarship of course. This way, I figured that I could continue to be the *nerd* I was but a more 'highly educated' version. I applied to a few colleges, got accepted at most. I also tried out for various band scholarship programs at each school. I picked the university that best suited my liking ... North Carolina Agricultural and Technical State University! Now this is where my REAL journey began ... stay tuned!

Age 19: Now I am a freshman in college! It was my first semester at North Carolina Agricultural and Technical State University! My parents helped me move into the dorm room that I shared with a fellow band student. With so many new things going on in this new and unfamiliar environment, I didn't know where to put my focus.

Trying to juggle eighteen credit hours, an intense band practice schedule, my social life, "me time" and homework time; I was exhausted. When was I supposed to schedule SLEEP? Or find time to load money on my card to wash my clothes with this automated washing system? I felt overwhelmed with all the new responsibilities. On top of it all, I started dating. What had I gotten myself into? Not surprisingly, by the end of freshman year, my grades slipped. I failed not one but TWO classes, I broke up with my first college boyfriend, I dropped band and withdrew my band scholarship. I realized finally what was most important and what would affect my future more positively. Doing well in school was the obvious choice.

Age 20: Determined to get better grades during my sophomore year with a little *harsh motivation* from my parents warning me that if I failed another class they were not going to continue to pay for college; I entered my third semester focused and ready to go. I studied hard. I did not go out partying with my friends. I pretty much "lived" at the library and by the end of the year; I raised my GPA (grade point average) significantly. Things were looking up.

Age 21: Yay I'm 21! On my birthday I went to *TGI Fridays* to get my very FIRST alcoholic beverage EVER! I ordered a martini, took a sip ... Ewwww yuck. Waiter can I please get a sweet tea?

Back at school, my course work was becoming more challenging now that I was getting into the nitty-gritty that is mechanical engineering. I made it through the first semester of my junior year—I think there was one C that slipped in there but overall all I made fairly good grades. The second semester of junior year rolled around. I remember the first day of the new semester. I always want to make good impressions on the professors, so I came in a little early and sat down in the front row of my Fluid Mechanics class. As I watched the other students file in, I noticed a tall, dark, handsome, well-dressed and may I add *buff* individual. He chose to sit by me! *Thank you! Thank you! Thank you!*

The professor entered, taught the lesson and assigned study groups for the semester. As if it couldn't get any better, the HOTTIE and I were assigned to the same group. Long story short, *he* asked *me* out. We started dating and as the spring semester ended *he* asked me if I would like to spend the summer with him at his internship. Of course, I said, YES!

That summer: In the beginning it is a little rough financially; we didn't really think about how much money we should have saved to pull off our big idea. So, I spent the first week looking for a job around town. I went on a few interviews and landed a cool job as a beach lifeguard, in Myrtle Beach, SC.

Meanwhile, *the boyfriend* was networking and pulling strings to get me a paid summer internship where he worked. After a LONG week of working in the hot summer sun, I received a call from International Paper asking if I would be interested in taking a summer internship position with them. Now that we were both working as engineers, we were not broke anymore and had a fun time exploring South Carolina for the rest of that summer.

Age 22: It is senior year!! I was passionately ready to be done with school! No more annoying professors to deal with. No more dorm rooms and roommates. I was ready to graduate and to get out of here. Senior year was definitely my hardest academic year. My courses included:

- Senior Design I&II,
- Computer Aided Design,
- Heat Transfer,
- Internal Combustion Engines,
- Flight Vehicle Performance,
- Mechanical Engineering Lab III&IV and
- Vibrations

The year was rough but I made it through and graduated with my class in 2013! It was a joyous day! I was done with school! Now what?!?!

Age 23: With no job to report to, I went home to live with my family until I figured something out. I knew that I wanted my first job to be related to the automotive industry—it was the one thing that brought me to college in the first place. So I applied to as many related jobs as possible. With my persistence I got an interview to do some temporary engineering contract work on large mining truck-axles at Caterpillar. I accepted the offer and did some good work. I even got two raises during my six-month contract!

I wanted to continue my growth as an engineer and not limit my skill-set to just one temporary job, so I searched for other opportunities in the area. I ended up landing an interview with Deere-Hitachi for a different engineering contract position. I accepted their offer and have been working at Deere-Hitachi ever since. I also submitted an application to speak as a presenter at the Society of Women Engineer's (SWE) national conference. The abstract for my talk was accepted over six-hundred other applicants!

Age 24: In just few weeks I will be flying out to Los Angeles to give my BIG speech at the SWE conference. I recently turned twenty-four. At work, I wore a big "happy birthday" pin on my shirt. I checked my e-mail that day and discovered that I had been asked to volunteer with the Piedmont Triad's (That's the name of the area that I live in.) FIRST—ever All-Girls Girl Scout Robotics Team! What a present and honor!

I was and still am super excited and feel good about what is to come. I am finally 24! And I made it for sure! Wish me luck for many years to come! Thanks for listening to my story, God bless!

Gabrielle's Five Inspired Lessons

- **Lesson #1**: There is power in FOCUS.
- **Lesson #2**: Always plan for what CAN go wrong.
- **Lesson #3**: Just "Do it!"
- **Lesson #4**: Network.
- **Lesson #5**: Ask plenty of questions.

Dedication

I dedicate my *Unexpected Pathways* chapter to some special professors I had while attending North Carolina Agricultural and Technical State University: Dr. Waters, Dr. Saad, Dr. Dunn and Dr. Sun Yi. I would also like to recognize three special men that have always believed I could do it: Harry Conrad Bryant IV, Alvin L. Jordan and Bob Hart.

Gabrielle J. Jordan Construction Industry

www.linkedin.com/in/gabbyjordan
gjjordan88@yahoo.com

Editor's note: Gabrielle did so well during her talk in L.A. addressing the Society of Women Engineers that she has been asked to give multiple talks at universities all over the country.

Inspiration and Introspection

Anne Sourbeer Morris, Ed.D.

There is power in learning about the experiences of those who have lived the adventures upon which we are about to embark. While we might not always heed the advice of others, seeds of wisdom may be planted. When I served as a Director of School Counseling, our graduates were routinely "invited back" to share their post-secondary experiences and to offer "success tips" to high school students. The students were mesmerized by the stories and advice related by the graduates. Although the advice frequently echoed that given by teachers, counselors and parents; the students were open to hearing the advice of their peers … When the mind is ready, a teacher appears!

Be inspired to make a difference … Even a small gesture of care may create lasting hope!

While parents are the number one influence on an individual's career choice, the support offered by mentors is critical. Mentors appear in myriad forms. As you will read, many of the *Women of Unexpected Pathways* honor the mentors in their lives—the individuals who believed in and supported them unconditionally. Gabrielle honored her parents and educational mentors via her story and in turn has become a mentor by example and deed. As a woman who has embarked upon a career pathway identified as non-traditional by gender—engineering—Gabrielle is demonstrating by example, that women may be highly successful in male-dominated career pathways. She also shares her time and talent by mentoring young women through volunteer work with SWE, Girl Scouts of America and *NC First Robotics*, the Piedmont Triad's FIRST All-Girls Robotics Team.

Careers have no gender.

Unexpected Reflections

What insights or enlightenment have you, the reader, gained from Gabrielle's chapter?

Journeys in the Fourth Life Decade

The Thirties

Chapter 3

START NOW: Four Undeniable Laws to Being What You Want to Become

Molly L. Nece

We all have been told life is full of opportunity. It is what we do today that matters tomorrow. Your pathway is unexpected, but that doesn't mean there won't be signs along the way. Keep your eyes wide open, heart pumping and mind growing. We've all won the lottery of life. It's up to us how we are going to spend it! —**Molly L. Nece**

As I sit and reflect on where I have been, where I am and where I am going, there is no doubt there have been four undeniable laws in my life that helped me become what I wanted to be. Perhaps the story of my journey may seem to be a little confusing, but as the decades passed, I slowly un-school myself. My ultimate *destination* became a little less important and the *moments* in that journey became more important than life itself at times.

Law #1: Build Your Legacy.

If I were to roll back twenty years to my senior year in high school, there would be many moments that didn't mean then what they do to me today—from coming in third place in a talent show for singing; to being chosen to deliver my "sexual overtones in advertising" speech in front of the entire school; to being selected as prom queen, having never once been nominated on any homecoming court; then being accepted to Gettysburg College to pursue my dream of becoming an elementary school teacher. While all four series of events came to me as a surprise, at the time it was pure jubilation. Looking back on that pivotal year, I am sure that these events helped to build my courage to try new things, gain the confidence in knowing that kindness pays more dividends than any stock and although my SAT scores were not the best, I was the one who would always make things happen.

Through my college years, three internships resulted in three transformational experiences that guided me in directions other than becoming a school teacher. Shadowing a psychiatrist in a hospital setting resulted in patients telling me not to leave because of how they felt in my presence. Shadowing a school counselor resulted in my mentoring a young teen whose mother was brutally murdered by her father; and running a weekly afterschool program at a church for children who didn't have a safe place to call home resulted in my ability to create trusting places. Then, when I won *Student Teacher of the Year,* deep down in my soul I knew there was something stirring inside me telling me to do more than teach twenty-five students a year ... but more of what?

After graduating from college, I remember praying for a letter to come in the mail. It would tell me who I would marry, where I would live and what I was going to be when I grew up. In my mind, I was already "grown up" and didn't understand why my life wasn't more clear. I would pray to God to show me signs. I would ask him questions and then look into a candle and ask him to make it flicker once for "yes" and flicker twice for "no." Looking back it may have seemed silly, but was it? Perhaps my intentionality was what eventually helped me accept that I'm not going to have all the answers and the importance to listen to others, but always to seek my own truth.

The questions still remained. Do I want to make a ton of money... then how? Do I want to help people ... then who? Did I want both ... then what? Luckily, I had a great mentor at the Gettysburg College Admissions Office. I was a tour guide, but I would also help her with special projects. I was in my element. I enjoyed being around the other staff members. I helped guide student's decisions as to whether Gettysburg would be a good fit, and put parent's concerns at ease. Working in admissions and higher education was going to be the place for me—at least for five of the next twenty years. After a short stay in corporate America when I chased the almighty dollar with big monetary gains, but very little enjoyment and satisfaction—I knew that a college campus was the place for me. To my disappointment, it took me by surprise that I no longer found fulfillment in the field of admissions at the next university. I found myself at the same place after graduating from Gettysburg five years earlier—feeling lost and waiting to be found.

It didn't take me long to refocus and take action. I enrolled in a Master's in Training and Organizational Development program at West Chester University. My love for teaching had come back around, but this time it was here to stay and it would morph into my dream job. I volunteered my time helping train staff in the areas of personal and professional development. I began being what I wanted to become. I was helping others find fulfillment in what they were doing and increasing morale at the same time while still working fulltime in the admissions office. The word began to spread across campus. As luck would have it, the Human Resources Office at the university was looking to carve out a training and organizational development function and wanted to grow their services rapidly. The rest was history ... or was it?

Ten years after college graduation, I was married and had given birth to our son. Once he reached six months, I began to branch out and get the entrepreneur itch based on what I had witnessed in our school systems—all knowledge and no application of what was learned. In pure Mahatma Gandhi fashion, I decided to be the change I wanted to see in the world. I never took a business class in my life, but I did stumble upon a brilliant business man who told me, "You have an idea. You build a business. Some will fail, but some will succeed and one loss will off-set the other." It seemed to make sense at the time and *MyInternshipGopher.com* was born. I partnered with a university faculty member who knew how to build a database system, and I knew how to build relationships, gain buy-in and support for a company that would match business' needs with students' interests done with a click of a button by schools.

When the economy crashed, so did the enthusiasm for the project. I learned the difference between buy-in and support. In this case, words didn't always translate into action. At that point, most would have tossed in the towel, but something was telling me to go to one more event for a final push. When I did, I discovered that the final push was intended for me to meet my next business partner who just happened to be a millionaire. I told him that I wanted to build his speaking and training company. He took a leap of faith, and once again, I was being what I wanted to become. That same business man who gave me the wisdom about building businesses when I have an idea challenged my reasoning behind why I chose to build his brand and not my own. I told him that I was following my instinct. He smiled.

A year after the launch, my business partner and I decided to write and publish a goal setting book in fifteen days in order to get it to market by the first of the year. Crazy ... Right? Nope! Just being who I wanted to become. Six months after the launch of the first book, I had built my speaking and training company with my own book in hand—*The 5 P Philosophy: Mastering the Art of Dreaming Big and Shining Bright*. My business mentor was happy to see that I finally stepped into my own spotlight.

Five years later brings me to today—November 28, 2013—Thanksgiving Day. I have not only written five books, but also renamed my speaking and training company to The Nece Group which now includes my husband, Dan Nece as a health coach and wellness speaker. Together we are determined to equip people of all ages and stages in life across the nation on how to lead, communicate, produce and be well in a complex world through our training and coaching services. We consider ourselves blessed to be able to teach, inspire and equip the nation with the confidence, courage and knowledge to step outside their comfort zones and create their best life.

As I conclude Law #1 Build Your Legacy, there is so much to be grateful for each and every day. Reflecting back on the past twenty years, I am most grateful for my persistence in uncovering my life's purpose and the love and support from my husband and son in that search. Choose wisely not to live by your resume, but to live your eulogy. Be who you want to become and make a difference, by being the difference!

Law #2: Live Your 5 P Philosophy.

After thirty-nine years on earth, if I knew then what I know now, there may have been a few less zigs and zags along the way, but I am grateful for the extra adventures it has created. My guess is twenty years from now I will be saying the same thing. That said, if I had a few less paths traveled, I may not be as impactful in the services I provide and the people I serve. I would like to share with you something I have come to call the *5 P Philosophy*. It has enabled me to know when I'm out of alignment and need to stop, reflect and shift. After all, we are all mere mortals.

The 5 P's are as follows—principles, passions, people, persistence and peace. Being aware of what is important to you will help to guide all future decisions and help to strengthen and nurture relationships with the third

P—People. For example, my principles are health, family, helping, adventure and economic serenity. If I am not getting the sleep my body requires, not drinking enough water and doing too much left-brain paperwork at my desk, it starts to show in my communication style and energy level. In my book, *The 5 P Philosophy*, you can take the principle quiz for yourself. I also recommend those you spend the most time with take it too. For instance, one of my husband's top five core principles is pride/self-respect. Early in our marriage I had to adjust my communication style because my words were triggering his emotional intelligence. Plus, looking back, I can take ownership for some of my poor choices of words. Our relationship is stronger because of this awareness and vulnerability we both chose to explore and continue to explore throughout our marriage.

The next 'P' is passion. I knew what I did and didn't like to do and how much I could tolerate doing what I didn't like to do and what part of the day I should take on the most undesirable tasks. I also realized that with enough persistence and a can-do attitude that I would strike a happy medium between my day job and hobby that would eventually become my fulltime job. In life, there is no space in the brain for what I call "monkeys in the brain." They run around and take you off your ultimate vision of success. There were plenty of opportunities for monkeys to enter my brain, but I knew that it was me who controlled my thoughts, words and actions. It was my duty to keep aware and persistent in achieving goals that led to living out my passions to the fullest. You must believe that one passion puzzle piece will lead to the next.

The third 'P' is people. There are a few people you may need to kick off your bus. It may be a little lonely for a while until you attract those you are seeking, but soon there will be people clamoring to get on the bus because of the brand you have chosen to build. Always keep in the front of your mind who you want to do business with and who you want to serve on your personal and professional board of directors. Don't forget to look for ways to serve others. When you spend an equal, if not more time, giving than taking, you end up filling up your heart, mind and eventually your bank account. Another *wisdom* is that learning doesn't stop after college.

If you are smart, you will continue to seek knowledge and look for ways to apply it. This is one of the reasons I decided to get my Lean Six Sigma and Mediation Certificate. In other words, ABL ... Always be learning!

The forth 'P' is persistence. So often people think fame and fortune happen overnight. The problem is they don't mix the persistence and peace together in their efforts. Peace is the final 'P.' People will say they are working hard, but is it on the tasks that will have them reap the reward they have specifically defined? Most of the people I coach are extremely hard working, but are not tracking the success of their efforts or identifying what success looks like prior to putting all the sweat equity into the process. Once peace is defined, they adjust and immediately begin to experience more success and satisfaction at work and in life.

Law #3: Be Your Brand.

The name of my first training and speaking company was the Molly Sunshine Group. People knew what they were getting with the brand—positive, forward thinking and goal achieving. It is either what my audiences and coaching clients were seeking or what they were looking for—others who already had acquired it and wanted to expand their network with those types of people. No matter what service or product you are providing, you must always *walk the talk* and model the way for others to buy into what you are selling. Price only goes so far! Credibility and trust are two things you must have in order to build a *sustaining* relationship. An inexpensive product or service doesn't guarantee that you are going to be able to keep their loyalty for the long haul in all economic downturns and upswings.

Law #4: Clear Your Clutter.

There were many people who gave me their advice over the years and then there were those whose advice I actually sought. Clutter could have come and stayed in my mind and heart that would have prevented me from getting where I am and where I am going. Once more, it is your choice to seek your own truth. Early in my career, there were those close to me who said: You are too happy. What advice do you have that others want? Don't you know training is the first thing to get cut? There were many more, but I chose not to focus on the *why not*, but the *what if*.

Family members used to criticize me for believing in the Law of Attraction. Today's society isn't built on hope and possibility. It's built on despair and fear. Today there are still those who say, Molly's just lucky. They choose not to believe the power of their own mind and actions. When I cleared a majority of my negative thoughts and people out of my mind and inner circle, the time it took for me to attain my goals was almost cut in half. That does not mean that I was operating in an unrealistic state of mind. I simply chose to focus on what was in my control and let go of the things and people that don't want to or can't benefit from my gifts and services. Someone once told me that everyone carries around a ten pound bag of stuff—some positive some negative—but it will always weigh ten pounds. Are you going to focus on the bag or where you are going to take it next?

The START NOW Model

To put into action the *Four Undeniable Laws of Being What You Want to Become*, I encourage you to take a look at my START NOW Model and stay committed to it over the next year. See what positive change you begin to see in your life. Remember, it is *your* job to create *your* best life. START NOW!

Stop the Mental Clutter
Track Your Successes
Acquire Skills and Support
Re-visit Your Vision
Trust the Process
Negotiate Opportunities
Organize Your Thoughts
Wow Yourself and Others

Molly's Five Inspired Lessons and Undeniable Laws

- **Lesson #1**: Undeniable Law #1: Build Your Legacy.
- **Lesson #2**: Undeniable Law #2: Live Your 5 P Philosophy.
- **Lesson #3**: Undeniable Law #3: Be Your Brand.
- **Lesson #4**: Undeniable Law #4: Clear Your Clutter.
- **Lesson #5**: Apply the *START NOW* Model to Your Life.

Dedication

To my son who is always looking for ways to make a difference, by being the difference, so that others can see that one person can make all the difference.

Molly L. Nece, Molly Sunshine Group

Training and Organizational Development CEO, Transformational Speaker, Life Coach and Business Consultant
www.mollynece.com

Inspiration and Introspection

Anne Sourbeer Morris, Ed.D.

I believe that people enter our lives for a reason and sometimes for *only a season*, as the saying goes. Some people, however, remain in our lives and in our hearts perennially. Molly is such a person. We met as she was launching *MyInternshipGopher.com* and I was managing a high priority industry partnership in Pennsylvania—this after I had completed a thirty-five year journey teaching and counseling in the public schools of Pennsylvania—primarily working with high school students. I found workforce and economic development fascinating and Molly was poised and ready to partner schools with business and industry—we were like minded—the *Law of Attraction* was at work. I mentored Molly and Molly mentored me. In many ways, she is still mentoring me.

*Seek the mentors in your life ... Mentors are ageless ...
Recognize them in all ages and at all stages.*

The truth is, I was inspired to find and share my voice as the result of becoming a chapter author in Molly's book *Sunshine Sisters: A Celebration of Legacies*. My chapter "The Legacy of Six," in fact, will become my next book! While I had much fear—Could I be an author? Did I really have something to say?—Molly's enthusiasm and encouragement empowered me and others to banish our fear and to convey our legacies.

Molly's journey again intersects mine—participating collaboratively in this volume and sharing her wisdom with you. Molly and the *Women of Unexpected Pathways* are entwined in my career pathway and life journey. Via their intimate stories, each of these women also touches YOUR life ... How will YOU receive the lessons offered? How will YOU move forward to touch the lives of others? How will YOUR legacy be revealed?

Evidence of your having LIVED remains in every life you touch.

Unexpected Reflections

What insights or enlightenment have you, the reader, gained from Molly's chapter?

Chapter 4

*A Diamond in the Rough:
Everything You Need is Inside of You!*

Latoya Rochae' Johnson

As you climb the ladder of success and always strive to do your best, there may be silence from the rest; just remember obstacles are only a test. Keep your vision permanent and learn to trust your instincts. —**Latoya Rochae' Johnson**

One day a little girl goes to the neighborhood park to find a group of kids about to start a game of kickball. She quickly runs towards the huddle of children and eagerly waits to be chosen for a team. She knows she is not the fastest or the most athletic but she always does her best. Just like all the other Saturday kickball games, she was the last one picked.

Fast forward twenty years later, the same little girl sits and waits patiently in a conference room for her group interview to start. She really wants the position and she believes she will be a good candidate for the job. While she waits, her mind wanders back to her childhood and she thinks, I wonder if I will be overlooked again?

Have you ever felt like you have been overlooked in life, whether it is in your career, in your home, at school or on the social radar? Well, you are not alone. It does not feel good to be picked last for the team but sometimes being picked last gives you more time to prepare for the game— *The game of life,* that is.

Are you a diamond in the rough? My interpretation of a diamond in the rough is a person who may not be fully developed in skills but has great potential to be successful with hard work, persistence and the proper guidance. A few years ago, I noticed a trend in my life that I did not like. I noticed that for quite some time, I was always the last one picked for the team. I often wondered if it was because of my lack of exposure, bad habits or my environment.

LIFE LESSON #1: SELF-EVALUATION IS THE KEY TO BECOMING A GREAT LEADER.

In 2010, I became a certified life coach and that is when my journey started as an entrepreneur. Before I sought out clients, I became my first client. I believe it is very hard to help others when you haven't polished yourself. I immediately took concepts that I learned in class and applied them to my own life. I wanted to give the world the best me.

In corporate America, there is a planning method called SWOT (Strength, Weakness, Opportunity and Threat) analysis. This tool is designed to measure the success of a business or a project. It reviews strengths, weakness, opportunities and threats. I believe as business women we should not only measure the success of our business but we should routinely do a self-evaluation on how well we are doing as leaders and rising entrepreneurs.

Self-evaluation allows you to grow professionally and stay polished.

LIFE LESSON #2: SHARPEN YOUR SKILLS AND BE PREPARED WHEN THE OPPORTUNITY COMES.

Preparing for the first day of school from K-12 is always an exciting time. As I reflect back to when my mom took my sisters and I school shopping, we never left the store without a box of #2 yellow pencils. No matter how many yellow pencils came in a box, if you did not sharpen them, they were of no use. This is the same way we can look at our skills and talents. Inside of us are gifts and talents some discovered and some undiscovered. It is easy to overlook your special gift when your everyday job does not require you to use it.

I have worked in banking for over ten years, but my passion is motivational speaking and youth empowerment. If I had not worked my gift outside of my day job, I would not have been properly prepared when opportunities came to me.

Do not let where you are define who you are and what you are called to do.

LIFE LESSON #3: SURROUND YOURSELF WITH THOSE WHO SHARE THE SAME VISION.

I can remember riding down highway 40 East, near Winston-Salem, North Carolina, and seeing a billboard for The Queen's Foundation, Inc. I drove passed this billboard many times and the message piqued my interest. I knew that I wanted to get involved with this organization and several of my close friends encouraged me to learn more.

Finally in 2013, I had the opportunity to meet the founder of The Queen's Foundation. The Queens Foundation (TQF) is a 501c3 nonprofit organization serving less privileged middle and high school girls in North Carolina with the goal of preparing them for higher education and leadership. The founder and executive director of TQF is Nadia Shirin Moffett, former Miss North Carolina USA 2010. I was very impressed with her passion for helping young women and was excited to get involved. I am currently a member of the Triad Leadership Board. When I attend the leadership meetings, I am always left feeling inspired.

When you surround yourself with those who have the same passion as you do, it ignites a fire inside of you.

Life lesson #4: Sometimes life will throw you a curveball but you are stronger than you think!

By nature I am a planner, but some things you can never prepare for. On February 29, 2012, my outlook on life changed forever. I donated a kidney to my sister. At that time, I was thirty years of age and some things I had planned for that year had to take the back seat. The process of becoming a kidney donor was very intense. For someone who is always on the go and very involved in the community, it was a challenge to be forced to slow down.

Sometime we get so busy that we forget to stop and smell the roses. During my healing process, I was able to regain focus on what was really important in life. Becoming a living donor was a very rewarding experience and it changed my life forever.

When life threw me a curveball, I was able to knock it out the park because I was stronger than I thought I was.

Every now and then life will give us a time out!

Life Lesson #5: Each season is preparing you for the next season.

The butterfly is one of my favorite insects. A butterfly's life cycle has four stages: egg, larva, pupa and adult. Each stage has a different goal. To grow into an adult, a butterfly must go through a complete metamorphosis. I believe the caterpillar is able to keep a positive attitude when it is in the cocoon. The caterpillar knows it will eventually become a butterfly. But first the caterpillar has to complete the different stages in the life cycle.

People may not believe in your dreams. Family and friends may not recognize your gifts and talents. To some you may look like a diamond in the rough. I challenge you to keep moving forward with or without the applause of others. We all must go through the lifecycle to success. Remember, you are a butterfly; you may just be going through your cocoon stage. If you do not quit, soon your wings will spread and you will be flying high up the ladder of success.

I did not know how my life would unfold when I graduated from North Carolina Agricultural and Technical State University. Ten years later, I am a life coach, author, living donor and a motivational speaker. Each life lesson and life experience has ordered my steps closer to my destiny. I started out unpolished, but with hard work, persistence and good mentorship, I believe I am starting to shine bright like a diamond.

Latoya's Five Inspired Lessons

- **Lesson #1**: Self-evaluation is a critical component of being an effective leader.
- **Lesson #2**: Sharpen your skills and be prepared when the opportunity comes.
- **Lesson #3**: Surround yourself with those who share the same vision.
- **Lesson #4**: Sometimes life may throw you a curveball, but you are stronger than you think.
- **Lesson #5**: Each season is preparing you for the next season in your life.

Dedication

I would like to dedicate this chapter first to my mother Rita L. Stitt; my sisters Renee' and Gina and my very talented nephew Jaden Johnson. Also I dedicate this chapter to my precious jewel, my grandmother, Ruby Jean Robinson and to my wonderful fiancé Michael McRae.

Last but not least, I want to dedicate this chapter to all of those who are pursuing their dreams. Don't give up, because it is always too soon to quit. You are closer than you think you are.

Latoya Rochae' Johnson, President

*Rochae' Life Coaching-Certified Life Coach,
Motivational Speaker and Quality Analyst
rochaelifecoaching@gmail.com*

Inspiration and Introspection

Anne Sourbeer Morris, Ed.D.

I have marveled at the common threads woven into the stories of *The Women of Unexpected Pathways*. The entrepreneurial spirit and the passion to make a difference in the world are alive in the stories of these women. The spirit and passion span generations. The spirit and passion are drivers of destiny.

Through her story, Latoya paints pictures to facilitate the reader's understanding and growth. Like so many others, Latoya is a teacher. She is gently teaching us—increasing our awareness that we are perennially evolving in our career/life journey. And, as we face obstacles, she teaches us that we will gain strength and resilience—if we will only take the time to listen to our inner selves and learn from our experiences. We *can* survive. We *can* thrive. We *can* move on. We *are* perennially *becoming*.

Finally, I must remark on the selflessness and generosity of *The Women of Unexpected Pathways* exemplified by Latoya—an organ donor—who put aside her own career and gave of herself both literally and figuratively in a most intimate manner. The giving of *self*—time, talent or resources—is a deeply woven theme present in the lives of *The Women of Unexpected Pathways!*

There are silent, often unsung, heroes walking among us. Take the time to meet them. Take the time to see them—to really see those who surround us all. Take the time to see the good in the world!

Unexpected Reflections

What insights or enlightenment have you, the reader, gained from Latoya's chapter?

Journeys in the Fifth Life Decade

The Forties

CHAPTER 5

A Way Paved by Curiosity

MITTIE DENISE CANNON, ED.D.

The construction industry needs women and women need opportunity! —Mittie Denise Cannon, Ed.D.

Growing up on a farm where my family made a living harvesting sweet potato plants, I quickly learned that my desire was to get an education and work for a company. With that focus in mind, I went to college and started on a path toward a medical career. My desire was to become a gynecologist so I could help women. Along the way, I took a job working in a toxicology lab with the intention of going on to medical school once I had a foundation to pay the bills. Little did I know at the time that this first job after graduation would change my career path forever.

I graduated with my undergraduate degree in 1992, and was assigned to a general contractor—by my then current employer—to manage an on-site drug-testing laboratory. It didn't take me long to notice the lack of women with hands-on involvement in the construction project. This single observation sparked my curiosity and redirected my passion.

Years later, I married an electrical engineer. I continued to pursue my interest in construction by obtaining some electrical books and teaching myself how to properly bend conduit, run cable, complete terminations and successfully accomplish many other related tasks by practicing in front of a mirror.

My husband knew of my excitement for the industry and eventually I convinced him to let me join him on-site as his helper. However, this agreement came with two caveats: [1.] I was to understand that a construction site was no place for a woman (especially not *his* woman) and [2.] Finding a company to hire us as a team was solely my responsibility. Full of passion, energy and hope, I started making calls. Each new company and advertised position led to the same result: "We're not hiring." When trying to practice my pitch with my husband, he explained these abrupt and discouraging responses across the industry. Like them, he felt that women didn't belong in construction and I wasn't fit for an on-site position.

Luckily, it takes more than a little discouragement to weaken my determination. In fact, this response was fuel to my soul. I requested a faxed copy of *Industrial Hotsheet*, which is considered a construction worker's employment bible, and continued my pursuit to become a tradeswoman. What seemed like millions of calls later, I did the unexpected; I finally convinced someone to take on our husband-wife team as journeyman electrician and helper.

With no time to waste, we found ourselves transported from Charleston, South Carolina to Baton Rouge, Louisiana. In my anticipation, I insisted that I have new work boots, my own set of tools and a new toolbox. Needless to say, I didn't know all the newness was a strong sign to the rest of the job site that I was "green," but you live and you learn. This was my first real construction job consisting of twelve hour days, seven days a week for up to sixty days. I was excited to finally receive answers to my questions about why so few women crossed the gates of a construction site.

Upon arrival, I was anxious to meet the recruiter so I could shake his hand and introduce myself. When we entered the orientation trailer, I found myself surrounded by men with tattoos and body piercings—something I was not accustomed to from my upbringing in a small town, Baxley, off the coast of Savannah, Georgia. However, I did learn early on "not to judge a book by its cover" and was not concerned about being in a room with these men as they were skilled craft professionals and were there to work.

Things took an unexpected turn for the worst when the electrical superintendent split up our husband-wife team and paired me with another electrician. The recruiter had assured me over the phone that I would work with my husband. I knew I did not have the true skills required to fulfill the position of helper. I had stretched the truth in the interview to get the job and now I was about to be revealed. I was in a panic. However, we honored the wishes of the electrical superintendent and I was paired with another worker. This gentleman made it perfectly clear that he was not accustomed to women in the field and he and many other workers feared that women would "take their jobs." My response was simply that I was there to do a job, safely, and to keep the client happy. This was the first step toward answers to my pending question about the lack of women in the field.

Of course, it was obvious to this journeyman that I was "green" due to all the shiny new tools that I was so proud to bring with me. We were given a specific assignment and the journeyman asked me to get a *skyhook* (a fictitious tool) from the tool room. Greener than grass, I went to the tool room and submitted my request for the skyhook. The attendant (and everyone else around) looked at me and simply laughed. I immediately thought *These people are ridiculous, all I want is the tool*. Before I could finish processing that thought, a male worker said, "Welcome to construction. We were all a green hand at one time and we know the feeling." This was my initiation into the field and I knew I had accomplished something great. Getting past the notion that men don't think women should be in construction and proving that I truly chose to be there and worked to belong, gave me the strength to stay the course. Despite the challenges, I did complete the project, an industrial plant shutdown, safely and productively.

After reaching this milestone, I had earned the respect of my peers and was promoted to assist the field electrical engineer. This mentor taught me how to read drawings and complete take-offs. As I look back on my journey, I am convinced that my pure curiosity led me to the discovery of my passion and purpose. That experience opened many doors in my pursuit of a profession as a tradeswoman.

My career took another turn a few years later when I was offered a position in workforce development with a different company. This opportunity grounded my belief that I belong in a company where women are unlikely to work, rather than in the medical field as I had originally planned. My calling was clear—I needed to explore the many ways to recruit and attract women to a successful career in the field of construction.

This unexpected pathway introduced me to great people who took an interest in grooming and developing me. Spear-headed by male mentors, the way was paved and I progressed from a tradeswoman to a leader in workforce development. Over many years, I have recruited and mentored several women, including the first female to receive top honors for welding in the Associated Builders and Contractors National Craft Championships. I am currently mentoring three women.

Over the years, I have received many accolades in the construction industry; I give credit for the opportunities I have had to those who have mentored me and also to those whom I have mentored. Through my work, I have been recognized as one of Birmingham's Top Business Women by the *Birmingham Business Journal*, inducted as a professional in Who's Who in Black Alabama and acknowledged as a business leader and champion for women by the Birmingham Women's Exchange. All of these praises are due to my decision to follow up with full dedication on my curiosity and the assistance I received from the many mentors and helping hands along the way.

As my career progresses, I continue to value education and delight in every opportunity to learn. Despite the career path change, I continued to further my education, obtaining a Doctorate in Educational Leadership. I truly believe the best tools in my kit are my confidence and willingness to learn. I've also realized that maintaining relationships with mentors and constantly networking are important building blocks for success.

Networking with other successful women has taught me how to survive in a male-dominated industry, to communicate effectively and to recognize opportunity. My favorite networking and continuing education workshop is the *Engineering News-Record's (ENR) Groundbreaking for Women in Construction Conference*. This is the most empowering event I have attended since my life-changing decision to become a tradeswoman.

Today, I am frequently asked to speak at state, regional and national conferences for educators, trade organizations and other groups. In addition to the national positions I hold on workforce development boards and construction camps for girls that I have started in the Southeast, I still find the time to give back and recruit women.

People are always the best resources. My networks and supporters are the personal and professional tools that I consider key to my success. Helping other women realize their potential in a construction career makes each challenge worth its effort. I am passionate about my career, the people who paved the way and those I continue to influence through my current position.

Mittie's Five Inspired Lessons

- **Lesson #1**: Never give up—Passion fuels your soul.
- **Lesson #2**: Always seek out opportunities for learning—Enter every situation with a learning attitude.
- **Lesson #3**: Learn from the mistakes of others—Take note of the experiences of other trailblazers.
- **Lesson #4**: Create opportunities for other women—Give back by helping others, that's how you get your blessings.
- **Lesson #5**: Learn to recognize opportunity—Attend workshops and conferences and pay attention to your surroundings.

Dedication

I dedicate this chapter to my family for their endless support and patience during my unexpected pathway and to my mentors for guiding and creating opportunities for me.

Mittie D. Cannon, Ed.D. Director of Workforce Development

Power and Industrial Industry
mcannon@robinsmorton.com
www.robinsmorton.com

Inspiration and Introspection

Anne Sourbeer Morris, Ed.D.

It is worth stating again. *Careers have no gender.* Yet, somehow women and men hear societal messages dissuading them from investigating the vast opportunities available, particularly in career pathways that are nontraditional by gender. There are tremendous benefits to women who consider career and technical trades as viable career options, for example.

Choices abound! Look around! Be inspired to chart YOUR course—to follow YOUR dreams! The journey to YOUR future starts now!

Nontraditional careers help to create economic self-sufficiency, as women attain high skills and earn the wages accompanying occupations requiring high degrees of technical ability. Women in non-traditional jobs typically earn twenty to thirty percent more than women in traditional jobs and over a lifetime, women in nontraditional occupations may earn one hundred fifty percent more than women in traditional occupations.

Having worked with high school students pursuing nontraditional career pathways, I observed that the students who were the most successful in navigating uncharted territory seemed to possess incredible resilience, persistence and determination often in the face of unwelcoming school or work environments. These students somehow navigated their way around, over and through societal barriers, as Mittie has—focused on her goal and her passion.

I wish that I could waive a magic wand to gift individuals the courage to follow their dreams despite the barriers—real or imagined—that lay before them. I wish that all students could have mentors like Mittie, who champion them, who teach them and who celebrate them.

Be inspired to be more than you ever thought you could be!

UNEXPECTED REFLECTIONS

What insights or enlightenment have you, the reader, gained from Mittie's chapter?

Chapter 6

Overcoming Life's Obstacles

Kelly Abeyta Jimenez
told collaboratively with Anne Sourbeer Morris, Ed.D.

We all go down our own pathways. All of our paths differ. Wherever your path may lead you, it is how you approach and how you embrace your journey—good-or-bad—that makes all the difference. Your ability to be resilient in the face of challenge makes you stronger and more knowledgeable. Your resilience and strength will be inspiring. —**Kelly Abeyta Jimenez**

Growing up in the early 1970's, in Pueblo, Colorado, *normal* was a family consisting of a husband and wife, children and a dog. Well my life was *normal* until my mom chose to leave. I was six years old. I felt abandoned. My mother's actions affected me so much that I swore if I ever had children that I would never leave them. I would do my best to always make sure they felt loved and wanted—that they felt special.

Despite my challenges, I learned many important life lessons. From an early age, I learned the importance of a work ethic. I learned that you must do what you need to do so that you can support your family. My father always told me, "You cannot depend on other people to take care of you. The only person you can count on is yourself. Through hard work, honesty and a positive attitude you can get through anything and accomplish all you want in life."

After my mother left our family, life was tough. My father was left to raise my older sister, younger brother and I. In the 1970's, it was not common for a father to be awarded custody of children. We were very poor and luxuries were hard to come by. Although we lived a very simple life, on occasion my dad would take us to Taco Bell and we could order one item from the $.39 menu. On Friday night when he had extra money, he would buy us pizza. What a treat! Sometimes, it is the simple pleasures that make life bearable. My father had to take on two jobs to support us and to pay the bills. But he always made sure that we had food on the table. We were together and we knew that we were loved.

At a young age, I had to learn how to cook, wash clothes and help to take care of our family. My grandmother also helped my dad to care for us. On weekends, we would often go to her house in *The Projects*. When we would stay with her, I can remember young men hanging out on her lawn smoking marijuana and doing other drugs. Although grandmother would try to run them off her property, she was generally unsuccessful.

Grandmother was a tiny, old woman who lived alone. We were afraid for her safety and for our own. My grandmother was a loving, strong and independent woman, truly an amazing role model. She was very religious. Grandmother took us to church every Sunday. This simple act of caring made a big difference in my life.

In junior high school, I was the ugly duckling, very skinny, awkward and tremendously insecure. Money was very tight. School clothes shopping happened only once a year on an extremely low budget. Milestones that go hand and hand with adolescence were also difficult to say the least—figuring out the hard way about deodorant, bras and feminine products was hard. I made it through despite name calling and bullying. I was pretty much a loner. I had some friends but not many. I took my first job in a sub-shop to help make money. My dad had to drive me to work because I was so young—age thirteen.

Finally, off to high school! I was scared yet excited and I thought that things might be different, but I experienced many of the same challenges that I had in middle school. Despite life challenges, I had goals. I always wanted to be a cheerleader or be on the pom-pom squad. I tried out freshman year, but didn't make it. My dream was not diminished. I did not give up. I continued to practice and it paid off! I made the squad during my sophomore, junior and senior years in high school! That achievement paved the way for me to start believing in myself.

During high school, I continued to work. I got a job in a jewelry store owned by our neighbors. I needed money since I had to pay for all my uniforms for the pom-pom squad. My dad let me have his credit card for a local department store. When I bought something, I paid the bill and started to establish my own credit. Watching my father work so hard all of his life, I figured I needed to start working hard for myself in order to *make it*, to be independent and not to rely on anyone for anything. And then my dreams grew. During my senior year; I was named co-captain of the pom-pom squad and was even thinking about the possibility of going to college.

Everything seemed to be going very well, when in October of my senior year, I found out that I was pregnant. Devastated, I stopped going to school, quit the pom-pom squad and wanted to give up. Voices from *everywhere* told me that I would not amount to anything and that I would have to go on welfare and be a drain on society.

Then one day, my teacher, Patricia Medve, encouraged me not to give up. She told me that I needed to finish school for my child and for myself. I am indebted to Ms. Medve to this day. Her encouragement made all of the difference in the world to me. I returned to high school—to a school for pregnant girls. I graduated, pregnant and all! I proved the naysayers all wrong. I never took a dime from welfare. I supported my daughter and myself by working hard and providing for us, with no financial help from anyone.

At this point, I want to interrupt my story to say that despite assumptions people may have, I was not a promiscuous girl, nor am I a promiscuous woman. Throughout my life, I trusted the wisdom of my grandmother, "Boys can tell you anything—that they love you and you are the one—but once they get what they want—they can leave you. Save yourself and make sure the person you are with is the right one." But ... at seventeen, young and naive, I made a mistake. I did get pregnant and yes I did wrongly trust what my daughter's father told me—that he loved me. We had been together for over three years and I believed him—I wanted to believe him ... but we were so young. For the record, I never regretted being a mother at eighteen. My daughter was and still is a blessing to me. I love her more than she will ever know.

Over the years, I have learned to listen to myself. I have learned that I cannot control other people's actions or make someone do something I want—to love me. All I can do is to control what I have the power to control.

After my daughter was born, my dad was kind enough to allow me to live in his home. It was difficult living there with my dad, step-mother, brother and two step-sisters. I was responsible for providing food for my daughter and me. I can remember days that I couldn't afford food, but I would somehow find enough money to take my daughter to eat at one of her favorite restaurants. I would buy her meal and she would ask me why I did not eat. I told her that I wasn't hungry, but truthfully it was because I couldn't afford to eat.

Unfortunately, my daughter's father refused to financially support us, so I, like my father, had to work two jobs. During those challenging early years, I focused my energies on working hard. I wanted to be able to move out on my own. I got a job at *Fashion Bar*, worked hard and got promoted to manager of the shoe department. Wanting more for my daughter, I approached my manager and asked if I could be transferred to a Denver store. My request for a transfer was approved. In 1990, off to Denver we went!

Because I still couldn't afford to move into a place of my own, I lived with my uncle. By now my daughter was school-aged. In my uncle's home, my daughter and I shared a room as we had ever since she was born. Every morning we would wake up early. I would drive my daughter fifteen miles to the babysitter so she could attend school and I could make it to work on time. Working retail was hard because my daughter would have to stay long hours with the babysitter. Many times, I would pick her up, take her to my uncle's home and then go back to work. I really wanted to get a traditional job—eight to five! I searched all over.

As it turned out, an opportunity opened up close by. I applied and got the job—a steady job with traditional hours Monday thru Friday 8:00 a.m. to 5:00 p.m. I started out as a customer service representative. With this company, there was room to grow, so I learned more about the company and moved my way up. With a good work ethic, I was promoted as Major Account Manager. I managed US West Communications for the whole state of Colorado—well over fifty-thousand paging units. On weekends, to make extra money, I worked part-time as a waitress.

Things were really looking up for my daughter and me. Then, life threw me a curveball. Although my daughter's father agreed with my move to Denver, trouble was brewing. In 1992, when my daughter was visiting her father, I was served with custody papers. To my shock I was not allowed to see her or talk to her. I was not permitted to communicate with her at all. I went back to Denver and to work. I hired the best custody lawyer in town. The story about getting my daughter back is filled with abuse and drama—I literally had to *take* my daughter back—but that is a story for another time. I will however say that the story is one of love and perseverance and the story has a happy ending. After a long and bitter battle, I regained custody of my daughter. After things settled down, I worked really hard. I made sure that even though I worked long hours and two jobs, I made time to attend my daughter's activities. It was rare that I missed something of hers.

Soon, I was promoted again—this time to the position of Customer Service/Inside Sales Manager. I began to make better money and was able to purchase my first home. The home was only a small condo but it was ours. My daughter no longer had to share a room with her mother. I made enough money at my full-time job to quit my weekend job. In 1995, I wanted to have a single-family home with a back yard and a garage. I sold the condo and purchased a home with a yard for our dog and a garage for my car! No more scrapping windows in the winter! Hooray! My life and my career seemed to be getting better and better!

During this time, I was in a long-term relationship. He was a great guy, loved my daughter and treated her as if she was his own. He was there for me through the custody battle. He also encouraged me to dream big and motivated me to be a better person in my career and personal life. But then another curveball, after over five years of dating, he stated, "If it is marriage you are looking for, I am not the guy." I had to let him go and move on like I always have.

In 1997, after being single for thirty-one years, I finally got married! I waited so long because I really wanted to make sure that the man I married was the right person. I always had the belief that you get married once and you make it work—you know, until death do you part. Marriage was great in the beginning. We were happy and my daughter was happy. I thought, this was it! I truly thought that we would be soul mates until the end. We purchased and built a brand new house in a quiet and safe neighborhood. I thought we had it all! Then, another curveball, this time pitched by the man in whom I had placed all of my trust. Infidelity reared its ugly head. We ended up separating and eventually got a divorce. I figured out that I could not make someone love me or be faithful to me, despite how hard I tried.

After working all my life I was jobless, divorced and stuck with most of the marital bills. Sometimes you think that life just isn't fair and that all of the bad seems to gravitate in your direction. I have shed many tears, gone through heartache, felt alone and felt that there was no way out. There were points when I literally wanted to give up on life. I was unemployed for many months. I was depressed. I knew that I had to look deep down, pick myself up and move on—I began to rebuild my life. I had to start from the bottom. I had to work my way up again. I did!

After months of being unemployed, I was offered a job—with a big pay cut—as a business development manager with a family owned landscaping company. I was starting over in a new business selling landscape instead of telecom. You might imagine the challenge of supporting my daughter, paying bills and paying off a mortgage—that pay cut really hurt.

I met a man in 1999—a man would end up changing my life. Our relationship started out as friendship. We were both going through tough times. He was there for me through my separation and divorce. Kris is a very kind and giving man, a lot like my Dad. He loves his family and is hard working. We had the same core values and beliefs. In 2013, after many years of dating, Kris asked me to marry him. And ... another curveball was thrown. A month before we got married, Kris lost his job. Kris applied for many jobs. We prayed about relocating, if it came to that. Finally, Kris got a job. The job was in North Carolina—so far away from Colorado. We decided to move. It was among the hardest decisions of my life—to leave my family, but we needed to move where the job market led us. We moved from Colorado to North Carolina to start a new chapter in our life.

Since coming to North Carolina, I have not had much luck with work—yet. I have met many great people and we were able to purchase a beautiful home—we are truly happy. We are supporting and taking care of each other.

As I look back at all that I have been through, I realize that this brief chapter cannot possibly break the surface of each and every one of the many challenges—loneliness, depression, abandonment, physical and mental abuse that I have experienced. I have lived in great homes and lived in the ghetto of Colfax—where there were shootings every day. I have been scared, hungry, exhausted and beaten up. I have been heartbroken and disappointed. But, I have always held my head high and have done the best I could in each circumstance.

Growing up without a mother, being a single mother with no college education was challenging. Ultimately, all I really wanted was to be loved and to be treated with respect. There are many people who have come into my life—who have helped me along the way. I am truly grateful. However, if it was not for the sacrifice, support and unconditional love from my dad, I don't know where I would be right now.

I strive to be like my dad and grandmother, hardworking and having the ability to love with all my heart. To me, it was all about the will to do better, to live better and to have a better life for myself and for my family. I helped in any way that I could. I willingly sacrifice for my family. I love them so much.

Today, I see my daughter having children of her own. Watching her lovingly raise her children is worth all that I went through. I see the life struggles that she has endured—a tough childhood, difficult teen years and the tragic loss of her first husband. Knowing what she has gone through, I tell her, "Do not give up. Dig deep and to fight for your family." Sometimes, we need to push our children not to give up and to be the best that they can be for their children as well as for themselves.

I have a good life. My journey has been one of perseverance, determination and faith. Yes, I have made mistakes, but because of the mistakes, I have found strength. In my strength, I have cared for my family and found love. I have experienced much.

When people think of success they may think that money is the answer, but when you come from nothing and you work to make a better life for yourself and your family, you may see life differently. I may not be *rich* but I have learned from my mistakes. I have integrity and I try to help out my extended family when I can. I am who I am because of my life experiences—good and bad. I have learned that no matter what conditions you are born into, that with faith in yourself, a drive to be better and a desire to show your children that dreams can come true; you can survive. I learned that I have to honor God and trust in Him. I thank God every day for everything that He has done for me and for my family. He has brought me through with love and grace. My journey continues …

Kelly's Inspired Lessons

- **Lesson #1**: Be strong, have faith and believe in yourself. Never give up on your dreams, yourself or your children.
- **Lesson # 2**: Don't let society or circumstance guide your life. Persevere through the tough times. Protect yourself by being cautious and respect yourself as a woman to not be taken advantage of.
- **Lesson #3**: Mistakes will be made … It is how you learn and grow from your mistakes that will make you stronger and become a better person.
- **Lesson #4**: Strive to be a role model … A hero for your children.
- **Lesson #5**: You are given one life—Live it and love with all your heart. Always take time for yourself, find what puts you in a *happy place* because you are worth it! You and I deserve to be happy and loved.

Dedication

I dedicate this chapter to all the people who have helped me throughout my journey: God, my dad, grandmother, Patricia Medve, Jacqulynn, Bellina, Adrian, Ian and my loving husband Kris … To Aunt Linda, my brother and all the family and friends who have believed in me and supported me along the way. Finally, I dedicate the chapter to my mom for coming back into my life.

Kelly Abeyta Jimenez, Stylist

stella & dot
www.stelladot.com/sites/kellyjimenz
kellyabeyta@hotmail.com

INSPIRATION AND INTROSPECTION

Anne Sourbeer Morris, Ed.D.

Words of encouragement and support can make a huge difference in a person's life—more importantly putting those words into actions can tip the scale. Kelly's teacher encouraged her not to quit school. The teacher provided Kelly with information about a school for pregnant teens. The information made all the difference and helped Kelly to graduate from high school. Yes, Kelly chose to accept the teacher's encouragement and advice, but what if the teacher had not encouraged Kelly? What if the teacher had given up on Kelly? What if information about alternate schooling had been *withheld* from Kelly?

Evaluate bias and assumption—meet others where they are in life.
Seek to understand first, and later to be understood.

Often we make assumptions that individuals know and understand what we know and understand. We make assumptions about their backgrounds and their life journey. We assume that others understand us. We make assumptions about the actions or choices of others. Because of these assumptions, we might *withhold* the very knowledge or information that the person requires to be successful.

Do not withhold knowledge or wisdom ...
Share your gifts to inspire others!

Like Kelly, many of the *Women of Unexpected Pathways* display great determination, persistence and perseverance—many of these women possess an incredible survival instinct. They thrive and survive in the face of adversity. The women are empowered to take responsibility for their actions, life choices and careers. When many might give up and understandably so, these women did not give up ...Why?

What makes the difference? Really, what makes the difference?

Unexpected Reflections

What insights or enlightenment have you, the reader, gained from Kelly's story?

Chapter 7

Caring is a Pathway

ANGELA LYNN JACKSON HOWARD

The only way to truly care for others is to take time to care for yourself. No one else can care about you, unless you learn to care for yourself. Caring is not what happened to you in the past, caring is a path! —**Angela Lynn Jackson Howard**

Mother was born Fannie Mae Jackson. When she was just two years old, something unexpected happened—her father left one day and never came home. Sadly, it was not uncommon for young black men to *vanish* from their families during the 1950's. However, my father's leaving changed the family and my mother's life forever. When *Grandma Janie* remarried and moved the family into a new house, one that they still own—just down the street from the local church and the cemetery—mother was sent from Texas to California to live with Mary Gentry, a friend of *Grandma Janie's*. A simple handwritten note allowed my mother to leave Texas and board a train bound for California and become the ward of Mary—a ride that changed Mary's life and mine. A ride that began a legacy of care giving—my unexpected career pathway.

Mary was the name I knew her by, however she had many others. Mary had been married four times and lived in three different states. Mary was very independent, hardworking but childless. Childless, that is until Fannie came into her life. Mary always heard that she could never have the things she wanted—a home, a car or a child. Mary left the doubters and disbelievers behind. She took control of her life and moved to a place where she could achieve her dreams and desires. Mary was a fair skinned black woman. While she was too dark to *pass for white*, her color gave her advantages in California. She could have passed for Mexican, if she had wanted to learn Spanish. Mary worked in homes, saved money, attended church, joined the proper women's organizations and raised Fannie.

My mom grew up in a small town called Riverside, nestled in an orange grove, seventy miles from Los Angeles and sixty miles from San Diego. My mother had every advantage that a girl her age could want; a closet full of clothes and shoes, plenty to eat and Mary who loved and adored her more than life itself. Mother went to school in a time and place where it would have been easier to just go to work alongside Mary, but Mary wanted the best for her. My mother learned everything that was required of her and went to church as well.

When mom graduated from high school, Mary was very proud of her. Mary wanted mother to go on to college. Although mother was a good student; she was much more interested in moving out of Mary's house and in with the man who would soon be my father. It surprised everyone that such a privileged young lady who was taught the virtues of marriage and who listened to numerous sermons on the depravity of *shacking up* would choose *that* unexpected pathway. Her choice, made mom unwelcome at her church.

After a couple of years, my father left for San Francisco to become a disc jockey. Motivated by a young toddler and Mary's many *I told you so* speeches, mom finished community college and became the first Black nurse to work for Parkview Community Hospital. She worked hard and did well. She purchased a home and a few cars, but never chose to marry. She was a caregiver. My mother gave me everything that Mary had given her and then some. I had a closet full of clothes, though most of them didn't fit me very long. I had plenty to eat and in most cases too much to eat. When mom worked, I was not by her side, because she worked at a hospital. Afterschool, without parental supervision, I became a *latchkey kid*. I also became a chronic overeater. Though an above average student, by the time I reached high school I weighed over three hundred pounds.

My relationship with my mother was not traditional. Somehow, mom and I became more like girlfriends or sisters. We even bargained with each other to kept secrets from Mary. When we planned vacations, for example, we were like two adults discussing likes and dislikes and negotiating options. We went on some wonderful adventures! We definitely did not have a typical parent-child relationship. During our last big vacation, we went to New York City. We ate at Mama Leonie's and the Tavern On the Green. We saw a show on Broadway—*Dream Girls*. We went to Ellis Island and toured the Statue of Liberty. While in New York, my mom met Robert Burns and somewhere between the Staten Island Ferry and a taxi cab ride home, the magic only found under a *Manhattan Moon* shimmered down on them. About a year later, while mom was pregnant with my younger brother, she had a devastating stroke. I knew my mom was pregnant, but Mary didn't—remember the secrets we kept? Mom just wasn't ready to deal with Mary's condemnation over a second out-of-wedlock pregnancy.

I should have known something was wrong besides a simple headache, the morning my mother had her stroke, because she gave me permission to drive to the store and to the pharmacy for her. When I got back from that errand, mom couldn't even sit up to take a Tylenol. The side of her face was droopy and the water just ran out of her mouth when I tried to give it to her. I called 911. The ambulance took mother to the same hospital where she had worked for so many years; later, she was airlifted to Loma Linda Medical Center. Mother was hospitalized for months.

During those months, I had to live with Mary. Though my mother provided me all the amenities she was afforded in her youth, I had none of the discipline and structure that Mary found necessary for a young lady. Well, over the course of those months Mary was bound and determined to teach me discipline and structure. First and foremost, I had to learn to clean. When mom was healthy we ate out, so there were rarely any dishes that needed to be washed besides cereal bowls. If we stayed home, we ordered pizza and ate from napkins or paper plates. Mary not only wanted me to clean, sweep, mop, do laundry and make my bed; she wanted these tasks completed on a daily basis! As it turns out, this "training" became the entryway to another unexpected pathway.

After high school graduation, I had fully expected to go to a traditional four year university and to live in a dorm. That opportunity became a distant fantasy. Caring for a premature infant—my brother—a disabled mother and contending with an indignant elder became my daily reality. At that moment in time, it seemed as if my world was coming apart at the seams. Little did I know that I was being shaped and groomed for caregiving; my family members were to be my first patients.

My little brother was an absolute miracle child. He was born at Loma Linda Medical Center in San Bernardino, California just one year after "Baby Fay"—the history making child who received world-wide attention for being the first child to receive an organ transplant from a primate. Though she only lived twenty one days, her experience saved my brother's life. All the media attention and interest in "Baby Fay" catapulted the hospital to become one of the top neo-natal care facilities in the nation. My brother, William, was born by caesarean section and weighed only two pounds and two ounces. He received the best care available and was ready to leave the hospital in only two months.

Suddenly, Mary had to prepare to take custody of an infant child and a disorderly teenager. She was well into her seventies at the time and had wanted to travel to Las Vegas, use her motorhome and enjoy her retirement. Mary never expected this pathway, but she accepted it. Mary sold her motorhome, to handle legal fees as she had to go to court to care for us. The social workers at Loma Linda wanted to put my brother and me into foster care because there were no fathers in the home. Mom was going to be hospitalized for an extended period of time with no good prognosis and Mary was not a blood relative. This time a handwritten note wouldn't do. When all the men in her life failed to do so, Mary loved my mother enough to stand up and take care of her children. She fought to gain custody of us.

After our court appearance, the appearance of our home became the next issue. I can't even imagine what the social worker would have thought about it before Mary came in to take over cleaning. She ordered us to purchase a microwave oven to heat bottles and get safety items for the electric plugs and locks for the cabinets. Next she wanted us to go to classes at the hospital. We had to learn CPR—Cardio Pulmonary Resuscitation and about SIDS—Sudden Infant Death Syndrome. Mary and I spent two weekends learning about little babies and the challenges they face in life. This was my first *college level* learning experience. Beyond all the things we were already going through, everything had to be prepared for William to come home. If ever I wanted a hands-on learning experience, this was it.

About six months later, mom was ready to leave the hospital. Somehow I was under the impression that when she left the hospital she would be able to return to her normal activities of daily living. I had never been so wrong in my life. Mom's permanent disability meant another full round of changes and challenges. The house needed major renovations including a wheelchair ramp and an open shower for accessibility. Mom also needed a hospital bed, bed-side commode and lots of help around the clock. Most nights Mary would take William to her house. I would stay with mom. I had to cook, clean and empty bedpans on a daily basis. Now that mom could no longer work, eating out was a thing of the past. Driving to the store, the pharmacy or a doctor's office were the only weekly outings.

In a way, I felt like my life was over and I would never enjoy myself again. It's only in hindsight that I realize by caring for others, I was really saved from many of the dangers around me. While my friends were going out and having fun, I was home changing diapers and assisting my mother. Thankfully, I also missed out on the gang violence and the drive-by shootings that occurred at some of the parties I so desperately wanted to attend.

After about a year, my mother finally qualified for her social security disability benefits. She was able to hire someone to come in and help care for her. I was ready to graduate high school, but it was evident, I wouldn't be going anywhere. The money that had been put aside for my car, our next vacation to Hawaii and college were all spent on the mortgage, renovations and health care.

At this time, a great young woman—Sharon—came into our lives. Sharon was a nursing student and an in-home caregiver. She was lovely, well-educated and kind. Sharon became the *big sister* I had always wanted. She took care of mom and gave me breaks to be able to see my friends or go see a movie. Sharon also helped me appreciate Mary more and realize that this time was really priceless. What Sharon was teaching me would be of even greater value later on. Sharon was right. I did learn a lot—from her and from Mary. At the time, I didn't know she was a pivotal guide along my unexpected pathway—my journey of caring.

Relieved of the responsibilities of full-time care taking, I completed a two year degree and I met the man who would become my husband. Melvin and I were married in the same church my mom was pushed out of for being an unwed mother many years ago. Mary and my father even attended the ceremony without fighting! My mom and my little brother were both healthy enough to participate as well. At that point, I thought that I was finally comfortable to follow my own path. I went to work in sales, marketing and customer service. It was interesting and profitable, but not compatible with my values. Then my journey changed again. My husband became ill. I left my career and went back to school to become a nurse so that I could care for my husband at home. Melvin had Early Onset Alzheimer's disease. Early onset means under the age of fifty-five. Melvin was diagnosed when he was forty-one years old.

After eight years of caring for my husband, Melvin passed away. I never expected caregiving to become a career path for me, but somehow caregiving found me. Now I care for other families going through their own health care crisis. I try to give them the same love, care and compassion that Sharon showed my family in our time of need and that Mary showed my mother so long ago ... my legacy of love and caring.

Angela's Five Inspired Lessons

- **Lesson #1**: Love is giving up "trying" to do it all by yourself.
- **Lesson #2**: Love is letting the one you love make her or his own choices.
- **Lesson #3**: Love is stepping in and sacrificing for the one you love.
- **Lesson #4**: Love is appreciating the people around you.
- **Lesson #5**: Love is recognizing what you may think is insignificant, is very valuable.

Dedication

I sincerely dedicate this chapter to Jim and Amanda Gane, who have given me the very special opportunity to work with their clients and their organization to make life a little easier for families: one case at a time.

Angela Howard, C.N.A. II

Certified Nutrition Coach
thefatfighter@gmail.com

Inspiration and Introspection

Anne Sourbeer Morris, Ed.D.

In the epilogue, I pose a question that I have pondered while considering the stories of *The Women of Unexpected Pathways*—Does the life journey drive the career journey or does the career journey drive the life? It seems that the two—life and career—may be inextricably connected, even interdependent in a manner of speaking, as seems to be the case with Angela's unexpected pathway. Was Angela driven by default to a journey of caring or did her career journey ultimately reflect the essence of her true self?

Be inspired to make a difference ... Even a small gesture of care may create lasting hope!

While there are many variables to consider, the choice of a career pathway greatly impacts the education an individual will obtain, the manner in which they will live and quite possibly, the influence that they will have in their world. But how does one select a career? Do individuals select careers or do careers select them?

Maybe the true question is what lies in your heart? What is your passion?

Sometimes our life presents unexpected opportunities for decision-making. We are presented with challenges resulting in decisions about the career or life pathway we might follow.

It seems that life—our environment and our experience—gives us clues about the path we might take. As Molly and Mary Ann share via their stories, one must be open to *hearing* those clues. Angela also took clues and learnings from her environment. Ultimately, Angela set upon a career pathway that, while seemingly unexpected, was aligned with her being and compatible with her values—love and caring.

What do you think?

Unexpected Reflections

What insights or enlightenment have you, the reader, gained from Angela's chapter?

Journeys in the Sixth Life Decade

The Fifties

Chapter 8

Original Medicine

Wynne Renee Brown, MD, Lac

The opportunity to heal occurs within the context of relationship. No matter what career path you choose, what you think about and how you treat yourself and others is the most important medicine you can offer. —**Wynne Renee Brown, MD**

Grasshoppers were my constant companions growing up. I loved to sit outside and study their faces and watch them chew grass, transforming it into something that looked like tobacco juice. They would let me hold them to get a closer look at their overdeveloped thighs and feel the stickiness of their legs and feet. With them, I felt safe and they knew they were safe with me. It was in those times sitting with *my friends* that I decided I would be a scientist and a researcher. It is then that my soul whispered to me the direction my life would take.

Like most children, I was inquisitive, sensitive and constantly trying to make sense of my world. Being an only child and growing up in a family of primarily educators and people committed to community service provided a template for my future. I have heard that the soul chooses the family and circumstances that a person is born into. My family has been a blessing, providing the foundation for the perfect unfolding of my life's work and has provided challenges that have ushered in my own healing journey.

My healing process has been a constant mixture of events, my interpretation of situations and being able to eventually allow my soul to show me what is real. My beliefs about life and myself have been shaped and reshaped by the challenges all people face. I have experienced abuse, witnessed abuse, recreated the abusive patterns I learned, been the victim and the survivor. For me, these have all been roles that have allowed me to claim my seat in the human race. These roles were the lens through which I made decisions, interpreted people's words and actions and judged others. I learned that people have a habit of learning through their commitment to suffering.

Growing up in the south added an additional layer of suffering for me. My mother told me that I was Negro, Black and eventually African American with a little Cherokee and Irish. Being light skinned and with straight hair, with an aunt who had Caucasian on her driver's license because she "passed" was confusing. I was ridiculed by my Black sisters, left out by my Caucasian classmates because I was colored and discriminated against in the community because that was the way in the south. Biracial was not accepted and mixed was not discussed except in the stories of my family circle. I was often alone; felt isolated and turned to *Nature* for company and consolation.

My maternal grandmother, who was my first grade teacher, encouraged me to read. I found in books an escape from the harshness of the world and was able to foster joy by transporting myself into the stories and being there. My escapades in reading along with the gentleness of my paternal grandmother gave me hope for something better than my rare whippings for misbehaving and the cruelty I saw leveled on animals, insects, birds and plants. My mother was busy being a mother to scores of children in the Winston-Salem Forsyth County School system. I was her constant companion after my own school time and learned how to be an effective teacher and leader listening and observing her. She always told me I could do whatever I wanted to do. Little did I know that just being myself would be the most courageous and challenging pursuit I would need to master.

My father was the epitome of common sense. He had a big open heart, loved to make people laugh and devoted his life to serving his community. He was quiet and I identified with his need for quiet time while finding ways to be out in the world. He never wavered in his devotion to the church and I knew with him any step off the straight and narrow was just wrong. We shared a closeness that allowed us to sit quietly and enjoy just being together. Sadly, years of smoking unfiltered cigarettes and working as a fireman took his life. And with his passing, another door opened for me as he came back to let me know he was all right and would continue to watch over my mother and me.

As in most African American families, my aunts and uncles participated in raising all of the children in our family and extended family units. This closeness provided glimpses of what unconditional love might be. That love was shrouded in a backdrop of alcoholism that took the lives of three of my father's brothers and two of my mother's sisters. We were all helpless observers to the progression of such a devastating disease. I was terrified by some of their behaviors while they were drinking and I retreated further inside of myself to hide and to protect my heart.

The weight of just living was palpable as I tried to understand why people do what they do to each other and particularly to me. School and sports became my passion to channel some of my anxiety about life, spending most of my time on assignments while learning the rigors of competitive sports. My interest in sports grew, having listened to my mother's stories about playing marbles and then playing and coaching basketball. But it was different for me, as I recognized an attraction that my mother never mentioned.

With hormones raging and girls talking about boys, I was often wondering what it would be like to date a girl. I had loved women since second grade. I never told anyone because the subject was never discussed. I went out with a few boys and worked to avoid the dreaded kiss. And eventually, I fell in love with a man with a big open heart who reminded me of my mother. He loved to cook and he wanted, more than anything, to be a father. He was not deterred by my admissions of attraction to women and we eloped after my junior year in college. Getting married was a way for me to do what was *expected* of me—marry a man. Eloping was also a great way to avoid dealing with my feelings about women, having to wear a dress for the wedding and really not wanting to have a traditional wedding.

Meeting the man who would father my children also helped me to make that transition from living at home to being independent. I was at North Carolina State University for my first two years of college, interested in veterinary medicine but found the large classrooms too impersonal for me. As an introvert, being away from home for the first time caused me anxiety. I did what many students do and ate all the hoagies and drank all the milkshakes I could. I tried to be with young men by letting my hormones rule my actions. Needless to say I gained too much weight and ended up in the student health center for treatment of the aftermath of my misguided attempts at relationship.

One of the defining moments of my life happened when I was in the student health center to address my anxiety. The doctor, a woman whose first name was the same as my cousin Nina, asked what I wanted to do when I finished school. I told her I wanted to be a doctor. At that point I was in my second year of college, skipping class, depressed, anxious, thinking about drugs and barely making a 2.0 grade average. She told me I would NEVER be a doctor and wrote me a prescription for an anti-anxiety medication. I remember thinking that she didn't know me and that I would prove her wrong.

With my grades falling after having been an honor student in high school, my mother talked to one of her best friends from high school who was working at Winston-Salem State University and was the director of an academic program in the health sciences for students interested in medicine or dentistry. She suggested I transfer and join her program. I did just that after completing my sophomore year at North Carolina State. I moved back home.

It did not take long for me to be interested in school again. The small group of students in Dr. Atkinson's lab also made it easier for me to make friends. With a smaller campus, skipping class brought consequences. I decided not to go to my Spanish class one day and wouldn't you know it, I ran right into my instructor on campus. She questioned me about my absence and let me know in no uncertain terms that she expected me to show up. That encounter changed something in me. I could see she cared about whether I would "make it" or not. That kind of concern for students along with Dr. Atkinson's close supervision and instruction helped me to be an A student the last two years of college.

Because of Dr. Atkinson's connections, I learned about an opportunity at the University of North Carolina in Chapel Hill, to take introductory medical or dental classes in a summer program. I applied and was accepted. The anatomy, microbiology and biochemistry classes, while challenging, ignited a fierce desire to master my studies and opened a view of higher education for me. I made a firm decision to pursue medicine after I failed miserably in the dental lab. Our assignment was simple—to mix amalgam, the same compound used for fillings in teeth and put it in the impressions of teeth we had made. Time after time, my amalgam solidified into something as hard as cement before I was able to get it into the impression. I concluded I would never be able to fill teeth. Not taking the failure as a loss, I simply crossed dentistry off my career list and by default, made becoming a physician my final goal in this part of my journey.

My goal in applying to medical school was to get accepted somewhere that would provide me with some small community or family support so that I would avoid the anxiety I experienced in my first move. When I was accepted at the University of Pittsburgh, I was ecstatic. Pittsburgh had a small town feel and I had family there. Equally important to me was that no one had connections there. I was admitted on my own merit.

Starting medical school was an initiation into what had previously been what I referred to as an *Old Boy's Club* that women and cultural minorities were rarely, if ever, allowed entry in the past. While I was aware of the differences in skin color in the three of us in my class, I was more shocked by what I had actually signed up for. I had taken the Hippocratic Oath along with my classmates as a first step in our learning process. The sacredness of the oath was palpable but in no way prepared me for what I thought being a physician was about.

During my first week, I learned that my teachers believed that chronic diseases like arthritis, hypertension and diabetes, once developed, would naturally progress. There was no discussion of prevention or reversal of the disease process. I resigned myself to learn medicine while exploring what I knew in my heart must exist somewhere outside of this *club*.

This place of detachment allowed me to continue to be myself, not taking on the title of MD as a way into "godhood" that I saw in some of my colleagues. It also helped me to understand my role in a person's illness, clear that they are responsible for choices. These choices led them into a situation such as disease or illness, and that while I can facilitate their healing; I am not a fixer and certainly am not their god.

Riding on my mother's encouragement that I could do whatever I wanted to do has carried and sustained me in the journey. My medical school and residency in obstetrics and gynecology allowed me to learn about the miracle of life, to share wisdom with women and their families, to provide medical care in other countries while learning about their traditional healing and to be a part of the changes in medicine that support the relief and prevention of suffering.

Giving birth to two sons and being privileged to give to them what my mother gave to me has more than made this earth transit worth the journey. My own pregnancies and birth stories are a testament to what we as women, we as human beings and we as animals—a part of *Nature*—can do with support and with love as the guiding principle.

So much has changed in the short time I have been on the planet. I can see my birth through my mother's telling of her story. I have watched my sons grow from newborn to men, greeting life challenges with grace, while choosing to be who they are and do whatever they are called to do. When their father passed, I felt a growing sense of despair, as I understood more fully the role of a father for young men in a different way. I still see him in their eyes, in their mannerisms and in the openness of their hearts.

When I *came out*, we were divorced and my sons were young. My family roots were shaken to the core when I declared myself. Being the first in my family to be openly gay created a stir and caused the Christian morals of my youth to rage from how I would be *going to hell* to how I was damaging my children. Everyone forgot what Jesus would do. The storm passed with time as children have a way of softening the heart. My sons understood that I am and will always be their mother. And, I am now in a nineteen-year committed relationship with a woman. We have both participated in the raising of my sons and hers and have become an integral part of each other's family.

When I was thirty-five, I awoke one morning and my *Soul* spoke to me in the pause between realizing I was awake and before my mind became active. *What would you do if you knew your life was more than half over*? was the question I heard as a thought. I never forgot that question and it has been the fuel of many days when I might otherwise sit idly by and let life pass.

I remembered that question when I decided to pursue a childhood dream of living on a farm. My parents would take me to visit the farm my father and his seven siblings grew up on. They would let me stay with my grandparents for weeks in the summer. It was quiet there with only the sound of crows over the corn fields and grasshoppers on the sandy soil. It was there that I felt safe. When my younger son and my partner's son graduated from high school, we bought a one hundred nine acre farm in Pennsylvania, with free range chickens, goats and ducks. The farm was an efficient way for me to work through the effect of trauma on my life and to learn how to open my heart again and love without fear. *Nature* helped me to heal as I farmed organically, cut and split firewood and learned how to call the animals.

The farm was also a place to be creative. I studied and practiced acupuncture and expanded my healing practice. As a way to address the dysfunction and disconnect I experienced in my childhood, I co-founded the Original Medicine Institute for the Healing Arts, an educational not-for-profit that "offers a way of healing in partnership with the Earth, providing workshops and assisting organizations and individuals to achieve their highest potential"—originalmedicineinstitute.org. Curiously, farm life became more challenging as time passed. And then the call came.

The need to support my mother in her older years was a call home that I had not expected. My mother had always been fiercely independent. I realized that, as *Nature* has shown me, change is inevitable, and that for me to fully be myself, I would need to explore the possibility of returning to the place I left with bitterness in my heart. In my exploration of what it might be like to move back home, I learned that my hometown had changed. My memories were just that, stories I was holding onto that kept me stuck. The fear changed to excitement as we looked forward to a new adventure, a new chapter in our lives.

And for me, I am first and foremost myself. And like every other human being, I am a beautiful mandala of energies coalesced into a presence here on earth so that I can experience life and have the opportunity to grow through service. When asked by a Native American at an event, "Who are your people?" I answered, "You are all my people." To say that I am African American or Native American or Caucasian would only recognize a part of *who* I am, ignoring the whole of my being. I am not limited by the neighborhood and culture I grew up in. I am not limited by a federal recognition of tribal rights. I am not limited by what others think about who I am.

I am a mother of many and a daughter of many. I am an environmentalist, a writer, an artist, an acupuncturist, a friend, a widow, a wife and a lesbian. I am a conventionally trained physician who believes in the traditional ways of facilitating healing. I refuse to be put in a box to satisfy someone's need to perceive me in a certain way. I am myself, the sum total of my history integrated into whom I am today and who I am here to be. Cultural rituals, language and relationships are gifts that assist me in connecting with others. It is the journey to self, the larger self beyond the personality that is the road to healing. Finding your self is the best medicine to take. It is a way of wisdom and a way to fill the deep well inside that constantly needs to be nourished.

Wynne's Five Inspired Lessons

- **Lesson #1**: My heart is where I find the truths that define my role as a physician and my life as a woman with purpose.
- **Lesson #2**: Each of us is a beautiful mandala of energies coalesced into a presence here on earth to have the opportunity to experience life and grow through service.
- **Lesson #3**: As human beings, we are an integral part of Nature. We can do anything with Nature's support and with love as the guiding principle.
- **Lesson #4**: Cultural rituals, language and relationships are gifts that assist me in connecting with others.
- **Lesson #5**: It is the journey to self, the larger self beyond the personality that is the road to healing.

Dedication

To Charlie, the beagle who taught me unconditional love, that dogs are intelligent, love to meditate and deserve to be free; and to Cooper, my calico cat, a phenomenal teacher that has learned to transmit peace.

Wynne R. Brown, MD, Lac

Integrative Physician and Non-Profit Director
Original Medicine Institute for the Healing Arts
www.originalmedicineinstitute.org

Inspiration and Introspection

Anne Sourbeer Morris, Ed.D.

Awareness and understanding were the concepts that I first considered, as I reflected on Wynne's career-life journey. I think of the challenges that Wynne experienced first as a biracial woman raised in an era defined by racial prejudice and secondly as a woman who initially denied her inner being in an effort to live the life *expected* of her—adhering to the social norm—in a generation fueled by misunderstanding about sexual identity. How courageous are those who in the face of prejudice are true to themselves. How painful life must be for the individual who is not able to speak or live her or his truth.

It is my hope that readers will grow in awareness as they examine the stories of *The Women of Unexpected Pathways*. It is my hope that readers will open their minds to the journeys of others differing from themselves physically, socially, mentally, emotionally, spiritually, ethnically or sexually. It is my hope that readers will gain increasing understanding and compassion for the struggles faced by many on the career-life journey.

Be inspired to follow your dreams and to live your passions! Love the work you do ... Do the work you love!

Despite life challenges, Wynne's career pathway seemed to manifest itself from the dreams of her youth. Wynne listened to her inner self and followed her truth and her passions. Wynne drew upon the inspirations life offered her to create a career focused on wellness and well-being; helping and love. Throughout her journey, Wynne has been and will continue to be true to herself.

Unexpected Reflections

What insights or enlightenment have you, the reader, gained from Wynne's chapter?

Chapter 9

*Paving the Road to Hell,
I Found Heaven*

BONNIE DAWN CLARK

One cannot know what one does not know! Ask questions, especially ask, 'What should I ask you?' My costliest decisions in life, personally, spiritually, emotionally and financially, came from me believing I was 'right' and that I knew how things would occur in the future; all the while maintaining an ignorant attachment to being 'right.' I can either be happy and rich, or I can be right. I no longer need to be right. —**Bonnie Dawn Clark**

My parents raised me to place a very high value on formal education. My father affirmed I could do anything I chose for a career with the caveat that I complete an undergraduate degree before doing it and before getting married.

During the first month of my senior year in high school, mom found my birth control pills in my pocket book and began an aggressive campaign to force me to stop seeing my *true love*. This emotionally charged and terrifying day precipitated a cataclysmic change in my life and plans. Rather than choose to remain in a stressful home with a mother who demanded an end to my relationship with my *first* love, I accepted Mom's offer to leave home and relinquish my parent's financial support. I chose what I believed was unconditional love and autonomy over conditional love and subjugation.

I was fortunate to have a job as a sales clerk at a clothing store and a good friend who invited me to live with her while her mom was hospitalized. I had to transfer to another high school, and thankfully my friend was very generous with her vehicle. I was able to use her car to get to my job after school each day.

I worked, shared expenses with my friend and saved money. I applied for and was accepted to attend the University of North Carolina—Chapel Hill with a small scholarship and grant. I planned to work my way through college and graduate in three years so I could marry my *true love*. I originally wanted to be a medical doctor or veterinarian because I loved to promote health, but when I got a C in advanced chemistry in high school, I erroneously believed I would be unsuccessful in a medical career.

I never discussed my irrational fear with a counselor; I simply closed that future door. Looking back, I realized that I had been conditioned to avoid asking questions, to anticipate outcomes and plan accordingly. At that time, I lacked the self-awareness and maturity to recognize this in my behavior; I simply believed that I was *right*. Since then, I have learned one can either be *right* or happy, but rarely can one be both. At this point in my life, I choose to be happy!

My lack of awareness about my numerous possibilities and my irrational certainty that I could predict my future success colored many decisions. I sincerely recommend asking every possible question of anyone who may know the answer—to ask experts what questions one should be asking them regarding the subject of inquiry.

We cannot know what we do not know. To foster and maintain an attitude of curiosity and adventure, rather than conviction and certainty, creates the best possibilities for living a life that is truly worth living.

While at college, I began waiting tables in a Chapel Hill restaurant, before classes, so I could afford my half of the rent, utilities and food. I roomed with a close friend in an apartment off campus, and I rode my bicycle to classes and work. Soon, I learned how to earn more money by painting houses. I began painting with some friends and was amazed at how much more painting paid than working as a server in a restaurant. Unexpectedly, I was getting an education about the discrepancy in pay for traditional female and male occupations.

My first semester course load was twenty-one hours, and to complete my finals, I stayed up studying for three days and nights for the first time in my life. After completing my finals that semester, I got my first ever migraine headache—causing tunnel vision. I lost sight in my right eye followed by intense pain and nausea. My roommate took me to the student health clinic where they treated me and attributed the migraine to stress and my birth control pills.

I had elected twenty-one hours for my second semester but decided to scale back to eighteen to work longer hours and have less stress. As time passed, even though I still adored my *true love*, I was falling in love with my roommate. When my boyfriend came to visit me, I was careful to keep the volume of our passion at a respectful level so as not to be insensitive to my roommate who was involved with a man—rarely able to visit her.

I remember clearly thinking one day about my female roommate. "Our relationship is perfect. We get along beautifully, enjoy each other's company and we never argue. The only thing missing is sex." I was happy with the sexual relationship with my fiancée and completely unaware of any sexual attraction to my roommate. This new awareness of my compatibility and serenity with my relationship with this female friend—only lacking the element of sexuality—opened a new door of self-discovery for me.

I never shared my thoughts with my roommate, but noticed for the first time in my life, feeling jealous when she spent time with another female friend and did not include me. I had never been jealous of my boyfriend's relationships—a realization that caused me to reflect on what this meant for me, my boyfriend and my roommate.

The stress and strain of my course load, as well as the work required to support myself convinced me after three semesters, to move back to Winston-Salem, North Carolina to live with my *true love*, and to transfer to a local college so we could maintain a better relationship. Ironically, on my first day back in Winston-Salem, I had my first argument with my boyfriend. The argument led to the decision to get my own place rather than live with him. The new living situation led to our inevitable break-up, after my discovery that I was a lesbian feminist.

It took me seven years to complete my Bachelor's Degree in Sociology with minors in Psychology and Women's Studies. I realized that in order to be the professional helper I aimed to be, I needed a graduate degree. Frankly, I was exhausted. I made a practical decision to join the military service. By doing so, I could enjoy a living wage. Eventually the Veteran's Assistant Program would pay for my graduate studies.

Despite my best paranoid planning to survive the military culture, which would dishonorably discharge me for being a lesbian if I were accused of such, I was totally unprepared for the overwhelming sexual harassment and misogyny. My first two years in the Navy Annex of Washington, DC were a nightmare. I began drinking heavily to numb myself. Eventually I was able to exploit the fact that a *predatory* and abusive supervisor was married to get transfer orders to another base—the base where my partner was stationed. This transfer also represented a career path change from administrative work to computer science.

In the Norfolk area, we bought a house and enjoyed life together until my work environment became so hideous that I knew the abuse would damage me if I didn't get out. I volunteered to obtain a Master's of Science in Education Administration at the Navy's request and their expense. I knew that becoming a student would enable me to escape the abusive situation I had been enduring with decreasing success. The decision also allowed me to work in a different capacity as a Navy officer. To obtain my degree, I incurred three more years of *obligation* in addition to my initial six years of commitment. The extended service seemed well worth the cost to maintain my sanity.

During my time as a student, I become aware of areas of incompatibility within my partner. Since gardening was a creative passion for me, to avoid that stress, I began to "work on the side" helping friends and family members transform their landscaping. In my sixth year of military service, I embarked on a landscaping business with the intention to do this business when my obligation to serve ended.

My landscaping business flourished quickly. I reinvested all of the profits into the business and hired several people to work while I performed my naval responsibilities. Gradually, my business became more lawn care and less landscaping. I was less invested in continuing the business, so when I resigned, I sold my profitable business to a local person wanting to expand his business. I made the mistake of financing the sale to him without investigating his credit worthiness or securing my investment with a lien on his home.

In my last year as a Navy officer, Connie Chung interviewed me. I testified before Congress, and participated in a series of speaking engagements about lesbian baiting to sexual harassment of women in the military. I was horrified when I submitted my resignation. It was not approved. As an officer, I served at the pleasure of the President and our President at the time was pleased for me to continue doing the work of three civilians plus my military duties, since there was a hiring freeze in the federal government. After considering my options, I elected to gain weight in order to be less attractive to the powers who decide who stays and who goes. I had never been overweight and was ignorant about how challenging weight loss becomes.

When I was finally allowed to resign, I felt like a prisoner released from a ten year sentence. After my Honorable Discharge from military service, I traveled the country with my new love, enjoying the freedom of expression and adventure that had been stifled in me for most of my life. Randy Shilts interviewed me for his book about gay and lesbian military service members, *Conduct Unbecoming* and I narrated a documentary about this subject. I returned to my home state to start a new career pathway as a mental health counselor and social worker in Chapel Hill.

I began working as a substance abuse prevention counselor and taught at a local community college while pursuing a Masters of Arts in Counseling at North Carolina Central University. Life was wonderful in all regards, and when my partner graduated from a Bachelor of Social Work (BSW) program and was accepted for a dual Ph.D. program in Ann Arbor, Michigan, I had to decide whether or not to go with her. I decided I would. I began to experience very challenging work issues.

Over time, with the changes in the mental health system, my work became more demanding and less rewarding. I realized I was not happy in my work. The issues could not be resolved. This coincided with my partner dealing with her own challenges. She was a brilliant, high achieving woman accustomed to being a big fish in a little pond. She was now faced with being just another *fish* in a *big* school. In 1996, a friend introduced me to the network marketing company, Excel Telecommunications. I began to learn how to build a team of business developers within Excel.

For many reasons, my partner of ten years and I separated and I found I could no longer work as a counselor and remain healthy. I accepted a job as a company representative for EverDry Waterproofing, not realizing that it was a sales position. I was very successful in sales because I listened carefully and cared about helping people. I won the *Sales Leader of the Year* prize in my first year, earning four times the income I'd earned as a counselor. I began training to become a general manager for the company, planning to return to North Carolina and open my own franchise with EverDry, but that opportunity did not occur.

In 2001, I moved back to North Carolina to be near my aging parents. I was unable to find a mental health job that would pay my bills and began a series of disappointing jobs. With the financial collapse of my 401K following the horror of September 11, 2001, and my inability to find work that paid my bills, I withdrew my remaining 401K to build a house to live in and later, to rent. I began getting more serious about building my Excel business which became successful and grew.

In 2003, I read *Rich Dad/Poor Dad* by Robert Kiyosaki and it transformed how I think about money, and that changed my life for the better. I began taking the necessary steps to get educated about real estate investments and started acquiring rental property. I had the great opportunity to attend the *Peak Potentials Millionaire Mind Intensive* shortly thereafter and had major positive transformations in how I think about and relate to money. This training and the skills I acquired were life-changing and timely. I was introduced to the teachings of Abraham, as channeled through Esther Hicks, in 1996, and while the teachings resonated with me, it took me almost a decade to integrate those lessons into my daily philosophy so I could deliberately manifest what I wanted.

On November 1, 2004, I lost my Excel business and the residual income without warning. Thanks to the personal development and training I was engaged in, I went from a negative cash flow rental property, excessive debt and limited income in 2004, to having a net worth of over $2.7 million in 2007. I was honored to receive the *2007 Peak Achievement Award from Peak Potentials* and to be inducted into the *$2 Million Plus Club of the Enlightened Wealth Institute*.

In August 2007, rather than hiring household help, I chose to move into my parents' home to care for my dying father and my infirmed mother who had broken her leg. I was no longer able to engage in my primary income-producing business because my top priority was caring for my parents. I hunted for a legitimate home-based business that would pay my bills and found *Coastal Vacations*; an opportunity to sell lifetime memberships for the best wholesale travel club in the world, allowing unlimited wholesale travel. I worked part-time while providing full-time care to my parents.

Applying what I learned, I earned sixty-seven thousand dollars in my first five months of my *Coastal* business. In spite of the real estate bubble bursting in 2008, and the credit industry contracting, I survived with many of my assets in place and was able to focus full time on my parents' well-being. My beloved dad entered hospice care at home in January 2008. I had the honor of caring for him until his death; the day after Thanksgiving that year. The opportunity to be truly present with him through that process was a remarkable gift. Most people jokingly acknowledge that time speeds up with age; and I was no exception. The unexpected gift I received, however, from caring for my father was that time slowed down dramatically, allowing me to experience a profound shift *to be fully present in each moment*. Caring for my dying father was one of the most precious experiences of my life, and it entrenched my strong desire to be of service. I am very grateful for the continuing experience of being present in each moment of my life.

Bonnie's Five Inspired Lessons

- **Lesson #1**: Maintain an attitude of curiosity about all possibilities.
- **Lesson #2**: Allow yourself to enjoy the journey of this life.
- **Lesson #3**: Successful people have fears too; they just do not let fear stop them.
- **Lesson #4**: Allow how you feel in each moment guide you toward what feels better and away from what feels worse.
- **Lesson #5**: You cannot give of yourself that which you do not have inside to give, so nurture *you* first.

Dedication

For those who fear they got lost in the brambles beside the path, I offer this account of my adventures through this amazing gift we call life.

Bonnie Dawn Clark

Author, Trainer, Entrepreneur, Educator, Coach
www.BonnieDawnClark.com
Bonnie@BonnieDawnClark.com

Inspiration and Introspection

Anne Sourbeer Morris, Ed.D.

When life knocks you down, dust yourself off and get right back up. There are myriad themes woven into Bonnie's story, but tenacity may be the theme that most boldly stands out. Despite the pain, Bonnie, seems to land on her feet after every knock down—after every loss. The diversity of Bonnie's career journey was born of choice, circumstance, opportunity and the instinct to survive. Her career, as with all careers, was built upon a series of jobs. In Bonnie's case, some of the jobs appeared to be unrelated, yet each was considered and chosen in keeping with her core beliefs, values and passions—primarily helping.

Knowledge is power that no one can take away from you ... EVER!

When combined, the experience, knowledge and skill that Bonnie acquired over the years is vast. These assets will serve her well as she embarks on the next phase of her career journey. We are sure that Bonnie will live her journey—wherever it may lead her—to the fullest.

Invest in yourself ... Invest in your future!

We thank you for your honorable service to our country, Bonnie. You are an American hero. We salute you.

Unexpected Reflections

What insights or enlightenment have you, the reader, gained from Bonnie's chapter?

Chapter 10

I AM Living the Adventure of a Lifetime, and So Are You ... You Just Don't Know it Yet!

LINDA EISENSTEIN

The best gift you can give to someone who is hurting, from a terrible loss, is love. Love will help transcend that person from despair to a higher level where they have a chance to heal and feel happiness again. Love can never be wrong. Love is always the way. —**Linda Eisenstein**

I wish someone had given me the extraordinary advice, that I am about to share with you, when I was much younger. It would have saved me a lot of tears and heartache, but would I have listened? Don't get me wrong, I have always loved life. I saw the proverbial glass as being half-full. Sometimes, seeing the glass as being half-full, is simply not enough.

The first part of my career spanned over thirty years of my life. It all started at age twenty-one, working at the local racquetball club, giving lessons, introducing and creating the first wally-ball leagues on the East Coast in addition to selling corporate memberships. There, I met a small group of very special women who I am proud to say remain my dear friends to this day, thirty-eight years later. One of my fondest memories is the day they taught me how to ski on the expert trails, from the top of Mad River Glen in Vermont. Now that was an adventure!

One of my special friends and her husband owned a newly established metal company. They were looking to hire a "girl-Friday" to an existing staff of about six employees. I accepted the position without telling them that "girl-Friday" was not actually on my list of career pathways, but sales sounded great. I worked my butt off, and eventually *Inside Salesperson* did become my new coveted title. It was here, at this wonderful and crazy place, that I hung my hat for over thirty years! I LOVE hats!

My new boss, Craig, turned out to be one of the most amazing people in my life. And, wow! ... What an introduction to the corporate world! The first year or two were the absolute most fun that I could ever have working at a legitimate company, making *real* money. The employees were all very close in age and we really enjoyed each other's company. *Margarita Mondays* made starting the work week off a real pleasure. Needless to say, no one ever got sick on Mondays!

Unfortunately, as the company grew and the labor laws became more stringent, our special day of the week was phased out, but some other really cool things replaced it. Among them was *Doggie Day*. All the dog owners took their critters to work. The animals enjoyed a day of playing, being bathed, enjoying snacks and were treated like kings, while we enjoyed hotdogs and camaraderie in a carnival-like setting. Craig also built an area with dog runs where we could actually bring our dogs to work for doggie day care.

The company also became world famous for inventing *National Nap Day*. We told everyone that we started the whole *nap at work* trend. It was not unusual in those days to turn on the evening news and find *yours truly*, giving an interview *about why I need a nap in the middle of a work day* and *just how much more energized and productive I become after my nap*—pre-YOUTube!

Craig was always coming up with new ways to have fun at work, which was one of the reasons we all rallied by his side as we helped turn his dream into a very thriving operation. He is a master marketer and knows exactly what it takes to become successful at his career. He is also one of the most genuine and kindest souls I know, which is why he is also successful as a friend, inspiring leader, father and husband.

I could go on and on about the fresh roasted coffee that was literally ground that day on our premises, profit sharing programs, bed races and much more but really this story is about treating every day as if it is the adventure of your life.

You see, as a young person, I did not appreciate those wonderful experiences for the daily adventure that they truly were. Imagine if I had said to myself every morning:

Today is MY adventure. What lessons will I learn today? What wonderful people will enter my life today? What blessings will be bestowed on me today? And when these things do happen, please help me recognize them and be thankful for them.

Adventures do happen, to each of us, every day. Frequently, however, we are too busy multi-tasking, talking on the phone while driving, texting while were hurrying off and having fleeting virtual relationships. As we rush through our days, we are missing the most precious moments of our lives. Those moments are full of secret gifts and messages that are revealed to us by God, the universe, our higher self or other embodiments of love that we believe in.

Note: To help me to escape and to ponder life's adventures, I and others often take nature hikes to nurture the spiritual self. I have found this to be a perfect way to open up and receive a special gift. Oh yes, there is just one thing… I must leave my technology at home avoiding any device that will fill my head with chatter and keep me from seeing and feeling the magic of life!

Life's daily adventures may not always seem to be fun and interesting, of course. They may start out as something that we don't even want to do. In fact, the more we don't want to do something, the more chance we have to learn and grow from it. I try to experience everything with a smile on my face and a positive attitude in my heart. At times, I have been presented with an adventure that turns out to be very challenging—maybe even heartbreaking and life changing.

In order to get to a place of pure peace and happiness during our adventures, we need to experience myriad emotions. To know what absolute joy is, we must feel sadness. To know what true goodness is, we must experience bad. To know what real abundance is, we must first be without. Every emotion has a polar side. How would you ever be able to know what peace is without experiencing war? Could you ever feel peace in your heart without knowing what conflict feels like? Could you ever know what true happiness is without first feeling sad?

We are given choices on earth. The most important choice is what we will *do* with our adventures once we experience them. It's easy to be happy when enjoying a positive experience, but we may come away with little growth. When going through challenging times we may become angry, bitter and full of resentment. Sadly, we may remain in that negative state of mind until we wither away. The result will be pain for us and for everyone who loves us. Or, we can learn from our experiences, take responsibility for our life's choices and blossom into a beautiful flower which will flourish and bring beauty and joy to the world. I believe it to be true that "like" attracts "like." I believe in the *Law of Attraction.* If we have positive reactions to our adventures, then life will, in turn, bless us with positive experiences.

I would like to share with you the most challenging and saddest adventure of my life. It was the tragic death of my *little me*. My daughter Christina was killed when she lost control of her car and ended up sideways in the direct path of an oncoming vehicle. Chrissy passed instantly from a broken neck. When I received the phone call and heard those fateful words that night, it was as though I was inside of a balloon and someone pricked a hole in it. I felt like I had lost all control of myself and my little world. I don't remember saying a word, just dropping the phone and going into my bedroom, falling down to my knees and crying up towards Heaven. My heart broke into even smaller pieces when I realized that Chrissy was alone and that I was not there to take her hand in heaven, the way a parent should. I prayed to God so he would be there for her, because I could not. I know my Mom was with her in Heaven, and that was comforting. The only thing that has diminished the pain of this horrific loss is that I believe she is *home* now. For some reason, she had to leave early. I can't wait to find out why ... when she takes MY hand, instead.

Chrissy lived her life adventure to the fullest, more than most, here on earth with lots of love and laughter. She learned what she came here to learn, taught who she came here to teach, loved who she came here to love and did it just a little quicker than most of us. She left us with a bit of her heart and soul so we are able to continue to feel her with us and love her always.

It took me two years before I could look at a picture of her, without going into short term depression. I recently found a super cute picture of Chrissy—she is wearing the sweetest smile ever. I've strategically placed the photograph above my computer. I swear we connect each time I look up and see her beautiful face. She will always be with me and always be my best friend. We communicate often. Whenever I need a smile, I just sit at my desk and look up to see Chrissy shining on me like a star! Once you feel the pain of losing a loved one, especially a child, then whatever life brings to you, will seem easier. Create your adventures in your "favorite flavor"—top them with your favorite decadent frosting, throw some sprinkles on it and enjoy your journeys to the ultimate!

I learned that anger and bitterness will not bring Chrissy back to me. Those negative emotions can only destroy my life and hurt all those who love me. In fact, I even found something in which to be thankful. The fact that no one else was hurt in that accident is a miracle. I want my friends to know that I am "okay" and please don't feel sorry for me. The best gift you can give to someone who is hurting from a terrible loss is love. Love will help transcend that person from despair to a higher level where they will have the chance to heal and feel happiness again. Constant pity and commiseration will keep that person down and depressed and will do the giver no good either. Love can never be wrong. Love is always the way.

Take a lesson from Robin Williams and his close friend Christopher Reeves. After Christopher's tragic equestrian accident, Robin visited him. About the visit Christopher said, "He came here one afternoon and … (well) thank God I wear a seatbelt in this chair because I would have fallen out laughing … In the middle of a tragedy like this, in the middle of a depression, you can still experience genuine joy and laughter and love."

My chapter was completed a few days after the death of Robin Williams. To me, Robin was totally amazing in his ability to bring people back from the depths of despair with his comedic genius. His comedy was the way that he shared his love with the world and his light shone as bright as the sun. I wonder why Robin had to die. How this could have happened? I have reached my own conclusion. Perhaps he had used up his special gift on the rest of the world and didn't save anything for himself.

I am no longer doing sales for a living. I have embarked on a new adventure—a dream that started about forty-five years ago as a young teen. I remember sitting on my purple *shag* carpet and spending hours flipping through the fashion section in catalogs, the likes of, *Montgomery Wards* and *Sears*. I recall dreaming about my future wardrobe while playing *Beatles* and *Beach Boys* records on my hi-fi. This became my favorite pastime, dreaming about fashion. In my dreams, I always wore stylish-clothing that fit my perfect dimensions and made me feel great about myself.

Dreams they were. The reality was that I was a rather chubby girl who wore plus sizes. I have pictures of myself wearing short tight tops that were not complimenting my tummy at all and shorts that always rode up on the inside of my legs because my thighs rubbed together. My brother used to call me thunder thighs and I swore I would make him eat those words someday. Please do not try to find these very embarrassing pictures on line; I would be laughed out of the fashion world!

Well, I never got down to my dream weight, nor did I ever achieve an hourglass figure. You know—the "perfect" dimensions that all the beautiful models have and work so hard to maintain. No one has ever told me that I am "beautiful just the way I am." I had to figure that one out, all by myself.

Today, I look and feel great! Some of that I will attribute to self-confidence, some to the magical healing effects of Yoga and to the "angels" that teach it and the rest of it to a positive attitude. Somewhere along the way, I found out that beauty goes a lot deeper than skin deep. It literally comes from the inside and shines outward. Beauty originates in our soul and emanates from us in all directions, for eternity. The more beautiful we are, the more light we shine … The more light we shine, the more people we touch.

Now that you know where true beauty comes from, please let me tell you just a little bit about my *passion … Clothes Befitting. Clothes Befitting* is the name of my on-line-boutique. The name came to me in a dream. For me, it says it all. Now I can assist women worldwide, who may need a little help to choose clothing that makes them look and feel fabulous. When women wear fashion that suits their individual body type and personal style; their beauty shines through naturally.

I am full of appreciation, love of life and enjoyment for the moment. Being open each and every day allows me to learn and grow. I have said, "Good-bye" to my ego—no longer having to be right. It was a burden that weighed me down, but does not any longer. I am working on being me without worrying about what everyone thinks about me—I know they love me for me. I finally love myself! I am beautiful, I am strong and I am successful. I am abundant in friend-ships and love. I am balanced. I give as much as I get. I am appreciative for all I have.

I am so lucky ... I am at peace!

Linda's Five Inspired Lessons

- **Lesson #1**: Dream the ultimate dreams to live the ultimate adventures.
- **Lesson #2**: Life's ultimate adventure is when you love what you are doing and doing it with the ones you love.
- **Lesson #3**: Unplug your devices to recharge yourself.
- **Lesson #4**: If you are lucky enough to have wise people in your life, always keep your heart and mind open because you never know when you will be lucky enough to receive a golden nugget.
- **Lesson #5**: Put a choke collar on your ego, otherwise you may be spending the night in the doghouse.

Dedication

To my daughter Chrissy, who at a young age, mastered the art of how to live every day as an adventure and with whom I will be sharing my final and absolute adventure when ... SHE takes MY hand.

Linda Eisenstein, Owner

Clothes Befitting
www.ClothesBefitting.com
Linda@ClothesBefitting.com

INSPIRATION AND INTROSPECTION

Anne Sourbeer Morris, Ed.D.

We may not be aware of the journeys that the women living within our circle of life have traveled. We may be unaware of their joy, pain or healing. These women may carry scars—*invisible scars*—that are known only to them. We may make assumptions about the life they lead—possibly believing that they live life more fully than we—but we may not see the challenges or the burdens they bear.

At times, our bias or assumptions may prevent us from seeing beyond the superficial—what we observe or what we believe to be true. We may think, "Surely this woman has navigated her life and her career with ease," when in truth, the woman may be living with immense loss—loss well hidden from the world.

Live kindly. Live with compassion.

How many women hide their *scars*, carefully covering them ... presenting a brave face to the world while carrying on with dignity, grace and courage ... surviving in the face of adversity?

Thank you, Linda, for courageously sharing your pain and for generously sharing your love. You are "beautiful" just the way you are! And YOU dear reader: Know that YOU are "beautiful" just the way YOU are!

UNEXPECTED REFLECTIONS

What insights or enlightenment have you, the reader, gained from Linda's chapter?

Chapter 11

Entrepreneur as Artist— A Winding Road Embraced

Margie Florini

I hope to inspire and offer encouragement to others who may have felt like their life is a jumble of wrong turns or changes. There are no "wrong turns" in life. All one's past experiences are like "test-drives" and contribute to one's beautifully constructed road of relationships and adventures. —**Margie Florini**

Born into a family of six very brilliant and talented girls, I was compelled early on to distinguish myself from my siblings. I was seven when I decided that playing both the flute and the piccolo would accomplish that. But I didn't just play these instruments with the casual interest expected of a youngster. I was obsessed with perfecting my skill and practiced with fierce determination.

And I didn't stop there. I also pursued drawing, painting and handcrafts that ran the gamut from small to large. What fond memories I have of planning and creating parade floats, of chicken wire, papier-mâché and paint with my best friend, Ann Cantone! This was an annual project for me during the '60s—to enter the children's division of *The Fall Foliage Parade* in North Adams, Massachusetts.

To earn extra money as a youngster of just thirteen, I started my own house-cleaning business. The business was going well until my mother spotted the advertisement I had placed in the local paper. There we were, the entire family, gathered at the dinner table one night, when my mom shrieked with embarrassment after she saw her telephone number listed with my well-written ad. I can still see her steely-blue eyes looking across the table at me as she sternly said, "Margaret Mary!" Funny, she didn't hesitate. She did not look to scold my four other sisters seated there. She *knew* that it was my ad.

I was able to keep a few clients that summer, but I had to pull the ad. Guess she thought having a cleaning business was not a point of pride.

In high school, when I announced to my parents that I was going to pursue a music career and audition for placement in music colleges, my mother discouraged me. To emphasize her displeasure she gave me paints, canvas and paper—her way of pointing me to art. She also told me I was not good enough to fill the very few seats available for orchestral flautists.

"How will you support yourself?" she asked so often. None of this deterred me. I continued to send out audition tapes that I made on a small cassette recorder in my bedroom. I entered and won seats in many regional music contests.

Then, one wonderful day as a junior in high school, I got word that I won a seat in a respected national youth orchestra that would be traveling through Europe to perform in all the major cities. I was thrilled.

To my horror, my mother said I could not go. I never imagined this could happen. My mother just wanted me to attend a local art college, graduate early and become a graphic artist with solid job skills. She thought my music would be better as a hobby.

I chose a different path. Music. It was all I ever wanted.

Lesson #1: Go your own way and learn.

All through the highly competitive years I spent as a music student in college, I supported myself by teaching arts and crafts and music. How I cherish those summers I spent teaching at a performing arts camp in Sweden, Maine and teaching art to students at after-school programs during the winter months.

When I wasn't at class, in orchestra or practicing, I worked weekends and three nights each week at a hip and artsy boutique called "Celebration" which was located on Main Street in Lowell, Massachusetts. I had total creative freedom working as their window dresser, store designer and clothing consultant to women in their twenties, thirties and forties.

Graduation Day May 1978! I earned a Bachelor's of Science in Music Education and that summer I began my first full-time job—a dream come true—teaching music at Browne Junior High School (grades 7, 8 and 9) in Malden, Massachusetts!

At the time there were two other classroom music teachers—one was the choral director and the other was the band director—so I decided to develop a humanities curriculum that would help my students to see the importance of the arts and music in society.

Encouragement during these years came from so many:

- Lynn Leahy who believed a fifteen-year-old could run her business, "The Craft Cottage" and teach others the joy of art.
- Larry Drouin, my Beverly High School band director, who trained me to audition for advanced, exciting musical experiences and

helped me to feel the emotional impact of music in my life.
- Jazz musician and director Phil Saltman who believed that a sixteen-year-old could teach flute *and* arts and crafts at his creative and musical Camp Encore/Coda with campers from across America and the world. What unforgettable people and experiences!
- Lee Bishoff of the Lowell Jewish Community Center who made it clear to me how important it was that my art classes made both happy children *and* happy parents.
- Bob and Dick Spurr, owners of Celebration Boutique, who gave me the freedom to be me. I loved mixing '70s colorful clothes and accessories to create what people called my "jaw-dropping" window displays and ensembles women "just had to buy!"
- And finally, Principal John Wright and teachers Maria Jackson, Gerry Ruane and Donna Cantera, who helped me to become a serious, compassionate teacher for hundreds of students at Browne Junior High School.

Lesson #2: Encouragement, often from "strangers", paves the way for success.

In addition to my daytime teaching job at Browne, I continued to teach private flute and piccolo students in the afternoons. On weekends and two evenings, I sold designer clothes for salary plus commissions.

Just when I was moving smoothly on my life path, I came to a fork.

Did I continue on my merry way or take on the unknown "end of life" journey and care for my maternal grandmother—the strong-willed, intelligent and amazing world traveler—who was diagnosed with cancer? She needed care and it was her preference to be in her home. With no one else volunteering to live with her, I took a leave of absence from my school post and moved a few belongings—including my flute—to Grammy's home.

Those months with her were precious. I helped Gram in all ways. After dinner most evenings, we talked about her life while we played cribbage. I learned things I never knew about her as a young woman and a mother. I always made sure to keep the teapot full and have fresh baked cakes ready for the many friends who came to visit daily to make their silent good-byes.

Then, one sunny Sunday morning, Helen Bristol Fuller passed away in her big house—in the same lovely bedroom where she was born, eighty-two years earlier.

Lesson #3: Pause to learn profound life lessons.

When this sad, yet amazing chapter closed, I was left wondering, "How could one possibly jump back into a busy classroom to teach and tend to the needs of youngsters?"

Grammy's death made me think more about my life. Needing to leave my comfort zone to rediscover myself, I resigned from teaching, packed up a truck and left for Tucson, Arizona. No job was waiting for me. No family or friends were there.

To support myself, I worked in retail—first at a large department store, called Goldwaters, then at Cachet' Boutique. Cachet' was an exclusive shop for women that carried one-of-a-kind designer fashions from New York, Los Angeles and Paris. The owners trusted me to manage their business, teach "executive dressing" workshops and organize the run-way fashion shows. The shows, held at gorgeous spas and resorts, presented the season's newest looks to beautiful guests. The only thing the owners would *not* do was *sell* me their business.

Disappointed, I left and changed my course, yet again, when I turned thirty years old. I stayed in sales, but this time entered the world of Radisson Hotel sales and tradeshows. Now I was the one wearing exclusive silk suits and gorgeous leather 4-inch heels!

Radisson Suite Hotel general manager, Chris Lacey hired me to assist his sales department's number one sales person, Joy LaFehr out of Tucson. Joy later encouraged me to fill a vacated sales position. I took the offer and soon began working the West Coast trade shows selling the benefits of our properties to conference planners all over North America.

I loved my job, colleagues and my new found independence in Tucson. I also loved my tiny poolside apartment. The building was part of a rustic compound once used as an artist colony in the 1920's. Surrounded by the beautiful Catalina Mountains, it was a wonderful, serene place to wake up to each day.

Out of the blue, an old flame—my soul mate—called from the East Coast! Four months and four visits later came a proposal and a beautiful engagement ring. I said my tearful good-byes and took the long flight home to New England for our October wedding.

Life was blissful. I continued to work in the hotel industry for a few years—now with Sheraton Corporation, but felt that *restless feeling* growing. Joe, my dear husband, encouraged me to take some art classes. At the same time, I began teaching flute and piccolo, again to thirty-five students each week. Tapping into my creative side, and feeling a new sense of energy, I decided it was time to leave my job with Sheraton and go to art school full-time. I joined art associations and worked hard to build both my art portfolio and my career.

During my thirties and forties, I faced what some might call a "road block." To me it was a "terrifying, multi-lane highway"—a road filled with agoraphobia, stress and full-blown anxiety that seemed to go on forever. I nearly lost my way and my life. Thankfully, Joe was by my side with support and love. He helped me to find doctors and counselors who literally put me back together.

During this fragile time, when it was even difficult for me to drive my car, I was invited to share studio space with a painter. It was in the next town about five miles away (not bad if you don't have panic attacks!). To cope, I drove to see her on back roads—beautiful, safe and inspiring roads along the coast—to get to what would become my workplace, my studio.

In time, I was painting at the studio fulltime and growing a gallery business with two wonderful women—Joan van Roden, an oil painter and Kathy Connolly, pastel portrait artist and print-maker. We called our business Beach Street Studios.

As Beach Street Studios grew, my music students were growing too and moving on to colleges and universities. Every year I was saddened when my flautists graduated from high school and left our music world behind. It was a more joyful experience to see my paintings leave the gallery than to say good-bye to my talented musicians, so over time I stopped taking on new students.

Now I turned my total focus to my painting. This lifestyle change freed me to create some of my finest award-winning oil paintings, mixed media and collage works.

Lesson #4: Be fearless and take new roads.

When I turned fifty, Beach Street Studios was going strong and our art openings were, by some accounts, "the social events of the season!" Kathy, Joan and I invited different musicians, caterers and two-dimensional artists to share our "mosh-pit" exhibitions with us—promoting all on our colorful and clever Art-Card Invitations (masterpieces on 5"x7" post-cards). Encouragement plus lots of laughter and love surrounded us, and our precious Beach Street Studio flourished.

Then cancer struck not one, but both of my dear colleagues and friends. As they walked their long and difficult roads to wellness, I kept our business open, painting daily, but now, sadly, in seclusion.

I found it hard to continue painting my beloved landscapes. These large, sensitive oil paintings that I called "homescapes" took a steady hand and much concentration to tell their stories on linen. My thoughts often turned to my friends and the business we had so carefully nurtured and grown.

One night at 3:00 a.m.—typically my creative think time—I imagined myself painting with intense colors in acrylic paints—on larger cotton canvases—with sticks and rollers instead of brushes. These works would be pure expression—no thumbnails or sketches of places, imagined or real.

By 7:00 a.m., I was in the studio and set to bring this concept to life. What freedom I felt as I moved my arms in large movements to lay down the initial colorful marks, the "germ" of the concept behind the finished work!

In 2007, I was on a new road, to a new series of works.

And, by then, the great news was that Kathy and Joan were well and beautiful again—creating better than ever!

What about those contemporary, multi-layered, abstract expressionist paintings? My new paintings have been embraced by corporations and collectors alike. For this, I am forever grateful.

And my *Art Story* continues....

I have become the artist my mother felt I should be. Sadly, she died before I could hear her say, "I told you so!" And this would have surely made us laugh together!

In 2012, when the time had come for me to market *myself* instead of Beach Street Studios, the opportunity arose for me to work on a new project—a children's book written by my dear friend, librarian and author, Laurie Collins. Her sensitive bedtime story was best designed as I imagined quilts were made, in cut-paper collage.

The Pajamas of My Dreams was published that year and won a bronze medal for Best First Book—Picture Book category—from the Moonbeam Children's Book Awards, a national organization. The timing of that just couldn't have been more perfect. How wonderful was that encouragement!

This, my first self-published book, will soon be followed by a second, which may be called, *Pajamas, Too*! I am happy to report, that my work on this is underway as I write this chapter.

And so, this artist willingly turns down another new road.

I look behind me, in my rear view mirror to recall where I have been, and forward, to ponder what may come around the bend.

Lesson #5: Find a way, find your road and embrace new ones.

Margie's Five Inspired Lessons

- **Lesson #1**: Go your own way and learn.
- **Lesson #2**: Encouragement, often from "strangers", paves the way for success.

- **Lesson #3**: Pause to learn profound life lessons.
- **Lesson #4**: Be fearless and take new roads.
- **Lesson #5**: Find a way, find your road and embrace new ones.

Dedication

To Joan van Roden and Kathy Connolly, my wonderful art partners, who shared their talents and lives with me while we built our creative haven, Beach Street Studios.

Margie Florini, Artist and Illustrator

FLORINI FINE ARTS: Fine Arts and Publishing
www.margieflorini.com
Florini@verizon.net

Inspiration and Introspection

Anne Sourbeer Morris, Ed.D.

In the end, each of us designs our life journey and crafts our career pathway—living the life we choose for ourselves. While the concept is much easier stated than implemented, we often must step out in faith—journeying into the unknown, believing in our destiny—even when we are not sure what lies around the next corner. Despite our fears—and there may be many—we come to believe in the wonder of the journey ahead. We move forward when the desire to follow our dreams becomes stronger than our fear.

Be courageous!

As we live through life's generations, our experiences add depth and richness to our journey. And if we are open to receiving them, along the way we are given *gifts* by those who surround us … The individuals who become our mentors, our confidents and our friends …Those who believe in us and who help us up when we fall … Those who teach us lessons, those who caution us and those who show us love.

Receive life's gifts with a grateful heart.

While our pathway may ultimately be circular, as we re-discover our beginnings and our life calling, as Margie has; in the interim, as we embark on unknown pathways, we gain valuable experience and may discover our true selves.

Be free! Embrace the freedom that the expression of your unique-self offers!

Unexpected Reflections

What insights or enlightenment have you, the reader, gained from Margie's chapter?

Chapter 12

My Journey

WINIFRED QUIRE GIDDINGS

My deepest passion for personal freedom provides the stamina I need to succeed! The most inspiring moment for me as a Coach is: I am growing more every moment in my journey, walking my own talk, being the change I want to see in the world and being that teacher who is authentically living her truth through her teaching. —**Coach Winnie**

The first time I rode an airplane was in 1988, traveling across the Atlantic Ocean from Monrovia, Liberia to Winston-Salem, North Carolina. Though the flight was 4,745 miles in distance, the destination may well have been worlds away. I was twenty-six years old, with two pieces of luggage packed with several of my summer African outfits; two of my favorite books; two-hundred-fifty dollars and a letter for my uncle who was to meet me at the airport. I arrived in Winston-Salem in the winter. Bundling up and wearing three pairs of athletic socks did little to keep me warm against bracing cold and temperatures in the teens. Adjusting to the snow, the culture and an entirely new world left me wondering what the future would hold.

Whatever my future would be, I believed America would have that answer. Everyone back home knew about America. The VHS movies and TV shows like *Dallas* and *Good Times* entertained us. We watched *Soul Train* and laughed in amazement at dances and moves that were reminiscent of the steps we cut in Africa. These shows along with the pop music and the effervescence of *Coca Cola* created images of a country that was boundless with opportunity. Relatives' letters from the US and the occasional, overseas calls from them confirmed what we had suspected about the country. Also, what we learned in school gave us impressions of what was possible and we, as Liberians, had a preferred relationship with America. After all, Liberia was named by the repatriated slaves from the United States and the capital, Monrovia, bears the name of an American patriot, James Monroe. And we too, had a red, white and blue flag with stripes. Ours, however, only had one star.

I believed coming to America would provide me an opportunity I did not have in Monrovia, Liberia. The country suffered a coup in 1980, where the deposed president and cabinet members were summarily executed at the beach on the outskirts of Monrovia. Soldiers took over the country and plunged it into mayhem, yet our souls resisted the painful deconstruction of our reality. We continued with our routines of school, work and home, but our lives would never be the same.

Then in 1987, civil war broke out in Liberia. The war would continue for ten years. Reports of death and carnage from the interior flooded into the capital with waves of refugees. Ragtag soldiers and militias careened through the capital streets, high on a potent mixture of cocaine and gunpowder called "*brown brown*." They patrolled the capital hanging from the back of commandeered vehicles and open pickup trucks, waving AK 47's and firing at will. The radio, through streams of static, reported curfew at sundown and screams in the night were followed by corpses draped across the curbs and in lifeless heaps in the streets early in the morning. Rape of women and children, disappearances and abductions were the new norm. My seventeen year old brother, Natupi, was abducted by rebel forces and taken to the interior where he was forced to fight or be killed for resisting a direct order. And he was not the only one.

The University of Liberia where I had studied closed early in the civil war. The government saw students as agitators. My dream was to become a lawyer to help people secure their rights. After all, people said I had the "mouth" for it, so it was a natural fit. Classes were canceled. Student activities, campus newspapers and protests were banned. Soldiers took over the campus and had their way with female students. On one occasion, a soldier confronted me and grabbed my arm. I told him the only way he would have my body was to kill me. On the inside, though, I prayed. A neighbor who saw what was taking place, rushed to get my father. He came running; half-dressed and begged for my life. The soldier recognized my father and relented as my father was a well-respected and loved teacher in town. On another occasion, two soldiers near our house arrested me in the street for not following their orders. They viewed my standing up to them and speaking my mind as too great an offense. Then too, my father had to rush to my rescue.

It was at this point, my father and mother decided it might be best for me to travel to the United States mainly to keep me alive, but also to continue my studies. My family raised the money for an airline ticket and pointed me toward North Carolina. My uncle picked me up at the airport and brought me to his house to stay with his wife and daughters. He was actually an older cousin who had immigrated to the United States. Years earlier, his father sent him to a relative's house in Monrovia to attend school, but he ended up being forced to work as a household servant. Upon hearing of this, my father brought him into our pleasantly crowded house of eight to finish his high school and college studies. Since my cousin was older than we were, we called him *uncle*.

Within a short time, the welcome mat at my uncle's house in Winston-Salem got rolled up and I found myself looking for a place to stay. Somehow, I knew God would provide; that in spite of feeling alone, things would work out. Faced with being homeless, a lady I met several weeks prior took me in. She helped me learn my way around the town and also helped me find work at a local factory.

The factory work was a far cry from what I expected. It involved much heavy lifting and repetition. Also, the concrete floors and warehouse noise took getting used to. I worked the third shift from 11:00 p.m. to 7:00 a.m. The factory was off the main road and public transportation was a good three miles away, so I walked from the nearest bus stop to and from work. Occasionally a co-worker would offer a ride, but I did not come to expect it. Many of the co-workers, which included mostly Americans, some Liberians and other immigrants, had been there for years, in the same positions, with the same routines, week in and week out. This, however, was not my path.

Within a few months, I moved into my own apartment. I enjoyed cooking in my own kitchen and used fresh spinach to substitute for the potato leaves we ate at home. Most of my meals included rice, a staple in Liberia. I also cooked collard greens, with hot pepper, palm oil and smoked fish, just as we did at home. At first, I slept on the floor, but getting the apartment furnished one piece at a time brought me a sense of accomplishment and joy. At the same time, I had to learn first-hand that people—even some pastors and people that demonstrate caring—preyed on immigrants. I had to always be careful of my surroundings. I got street smart.

My school plans were postponed as the financial aid I expected did not materialize. So, I decided to work an additional shift to save up to start school. I worked two shifts at the factory and enrolled in school. Most of my units from University of Liberia did not transfer so I started my college career all over. I went to school, studied and worked one and sometimes two shifts.

A friend I knew from Liberia traveled to the United States around the same time I did. He went to Ohio to study. We remained in contact. Soon after, he proposed, we married and moved to Detroit, Michigan where he started pastoring a United Methodist church. My life was starting to go in the right direction. We had a son, named Joel, the love of my life. We moved into a nice home, in a great section of the city.

I continued my studies in Michigan and was able to complete the Bachelor of Arts Degree in Family Life Education from Spring Arbor College. In 1996, I earned a Master's in Clinical Pastoral Counseling from Ashland Theological Seminary. After completing an internship at a hospital's chaplaincy office, I received my license in counseling and also trained as a professional therapist. I found work I enjoyed in counseling at-risk youth, children and families. I also worked with group homes, managed several teams and poured myself into helping others.

Between caring for my son, running our household, managing the relationship with my husband and working a demanding schedule, I ran out of time for myself. At one point, I opened a mall retail shop to sell African clothes. In addition to this, I sold Mary Kay cosmetics. From both of these ventures, I made enough to send money to help my family in Liberia survive, something my husband never quite fully understood nor agreed to support. At the time, I felt I had to do all these things to take care of the people in my life, even if it was at my expense.

In 2002, my husband and I divorced. The marriage bed grew cold. The truth is that the marriage was over long before the divorce. We created two worlds for ourselves, though we lived under the same roof. We felt his career needed it and the image of success I wanted to project to the community required it. We tacitly agreed to maintain the façade and justified the charade for the sake of our son. And I continued to focus on my son and my family back home.

While in Detroit, I helped my family flee the fighting in Liberia and relocate to Ghana, two countries away. After a time there, I was able to resettle three of my siblings and my parents to the United States. Over three years, I hired an attorney and obtained visas for them to enter the United States. I helped one sister and her husband stay in Ghana, then Togo until their return to Liberia after the war. We could not find my brother, Natupi, for years, until a former student of my father recognized my brother and helped him escape from his captors. Like many of our veterans here in the United States, he was never the same. He struggled then and now with the demons of unspoken horror that engulfed him.

My family was always close to me, particularly my father. I was the eldest of seven children, one of which passed away. As the eldest, at age five, I fed, burped and changed my siblings. I babysat and washed diapers for a succession of siblings that seemed to come every other year. I learned how to clean a house, iron my father's shirts and make the basic meals for a large family. I learned how to play several roles at once: caregiver, child, big sister and daughter. My father, however, was my refuge.

Next to God came my father. He would come home from a long day at school where he worked and always ask me about my day. I supposed he realized the unusual burden placed on me by my mother. He made me feel special. The fact that he named me after his mother possibly fostered the spiritual kinship and closeness we shared.

Many of my life's lessons came from my papa. He taught me how to be true to myself. He believed in me and encouraged me to dream. He constantly told me I could accomplish anything I set my mind to. He taught me how to think independently and how to stand apart from the crowd. When he disciplined me for misbehaving or constantly fighting other students after school, he always asked me questions that made me examine my reasons and be accountable for my actions. He also taught me the value of discipline, humility and service by his own example.

Though I did not realize it at the time, my mother also taught me valuable, life lessons. She taught me perseverance. I never realized that my mother was not much older than I was—there were only twenty year's difference between us. She gave up her education beyond high school and her own independence for the sake of her children. The sacrifice she imposed on me as a child was a fraction of the sacrifice she made for my father and us, as a family. It was not until recently that I realized that my mother, at seventy-six years of age, not only likes her African attire, but also likes to dress in pantsuits and wear make-up, something my father did not condone. It was only until my father passed away, at age eighty-six, after fifty-one years of marriage that I realized my mother liked to flirt.

Though I worshipped my father, I came to realize that his insistence on accompanying my mother to her hair appointments and to her relative's house was not always about her safety. We also came to learn that my father had a separate family and another set of six children across town, a hold-over from the tolerated, polygamous culture practiced in Liberia. It had everything to do with the cultural tradition, unjust structures and manner in which women were and are treated in Liberia—as property.

Later in his years, I confronted my father about the "other" family. I also asked him how he could deprive my mother of her education, when he, himself, was an educator. He looked downward and said, "That is how things were then."

While my family settled in Maryland, I returned to Winston-Salem with my son, Joel. By now, Joel was nine years old. Winston-Salem was the town I knew and the place where I got my start. I felt Winston-Salem would provide me an opportunity to re-invent myself. It was a safe and decent environment for my son to grow into a man.

After the divorce, I only wanted my freedom. The court ordered child support, but it never came. When we arrived in Winston-Salem, I placed all of my savings to prepay the rent for twelve months. The threat of being homeless, again—this time with a child—was more than I could bear. Somehow we managed to make it. I received welfare, found work and started to rebuild my life.

I did some soul searching and decided I wanted to work with women by providing life coaching. Counseling and therapy work burned me out. I was putting in long hours, spending more time on administrative matters than client contact and fighting the issues of meeting upper management's cost mandates at the expense of client care. I took a number of training courses, obtained my life coaching certification and started Perception Matters Coaching, in 2009.

My friends and family questioned the wisdom of starting a company coaching women when I could work in my field of study. We had ongoing discussions about the issue of receiving a steady paycheck versus the challenge of breaking even in a startup business. This did not dissuade me. In fact, it encouraged me to go on.

I continued to build my business, to meet new people and sign-up clients. I accepted speaking engagements and held seminars for teens, women's groups and others. I felt honored to serve women using my skill, training, life experience and belief in them. From a faith perspective, I felt that if I could help one woman, then that would be worth more than anything in this world.

And my own journey continues. I take time to love and nourish myself. I set up healthy boundaries for myself and my relationships with family, friends and colleagues. I read and revisit books I have read through the years. My son is twenty and is at a point where he is finding his own way in life. My relationship with my mother is at a better place—now we can talk openly. We cry and laugh together. My business is growing, not without challenges, but I see its direction. I learned that as I heal, I can help others heal. As I grow, I can help others grow.

If I were to name three things that have sustained me in my journey it would be my faith in God, my father's love and teachings and my determination to make a difference in the lives of women. Though I am a long way from my first flight, these are the values that help me soar.

Coach Winnie's Five Inspired Lessons

- **Lesson #1**: Discover Who You Are—Learn how to develop a sense of who you are.
- **Lesson #2**: Increase Self Love—See yourself strong and not waiting for others to esteem you.
- **Lesson #3**: Be True to Yourself—Self-acceptance, be truly honest with yourself.
- **Lesson #4**: Have the Ability to Live Your Truth—Be transparent on your journey.
- **Lesson #5**: Be Assertive—Stand strong for your conviction.

Dedication

I dedicate this chapter to my mother, Weah Quire, the most important woman in my life. I also dedicate this chapter to women globally who are committed to self-discovery.

Winifred Quire Giddings, M.A., C.P.C.
Certified Professional Coach

Founder and President of Matters, LLC
www.perceptionmatterscoaching.com
coachwinniee@gmail.com

Inspiration and Introspection

Anne Sourbeer Morris, Ed.D.

Many of the journeys that the *Women of Unexpected Pathways* have taken were born of love—of someone's love for them, of their love for others or of their love of self. Love and the actions born of love and caring may change the trajectory of life. Love may ground us and enable us to move forward in even the most desperate situations.

I think of the love that Winifred's parents had for her, when they sent her to America in a bold effort to protect her and to save her life. I think of Winnifred's love of her family, as she fought to bring them to safety. Finally, I think of Winnifred's love of her son, as she sacrificed to assure his safety and well-being. Winnifred's is a story of love, determination, survival and deep faith. Winifred's career-life journey was built on the foundation of love and the desire to help others while helping herself. And ... *Coach Winnie* did it her way!

The *Women of Unexpected Pathways* teach us lessons. Their stories increase our awareness and understanding. Via her story, Winifred offers a snapshot of global events—a snapshot at which we may choose not to look. These events may seem to be very distant from our own existence. My thoughts are drawn to the people of Liberia who have endured years of civil unrest and violence—violence that many in America cannot comprehend. The people of the world are our neighbors on this planet—fellow passengers on this journey.

I pray for world peace, born of love.

Unexpected Reflections

What insights or enlightenment have you, the reader, gained from Winifred's chapter?

Chapter 13

Make Your Passion Your Paycheck!

MARY ANN HAUSER

If you are lacking the confidence you need to reach for your dream, it is possible to teach yourself confidence. Find a mentor, friend, coach who can help you to formulate your success statement that you can say to yourself every day until you just know who you are. Write your

'I AM' statements that will drive you forward. You can do anything you want if you put your mind to it! But don't do it alone, find someone to hold you accountable and the world is yours! —**Mary Ann Hauser**

I marvel about my family history. I wonder about the generations before me. I wonder how they might have—through nature or nurture—impacted who I am today. I'm fifty-five this year and have spent many of the years of my life wondering about my parents and grandparents—what motivated and made them who they were? What influenced them to choose their career? What legacy did they leave behind that I have drawn upon?

I never met my grandparents. However I'm dreaming that my dad's dad had business sense and that my dad's mom was a nurturer. I dream that my mom's mom had a farmer's spirit and that her dad, I'm guessing, loved to play.

I definitely learned about self-education from my mom; she was always reading. My dad taught me that *family comes first* and that hard work is important. My brothers and their wives taught me about raising a family. My sister won't believe it, but she taught me about forgiveness.

I know that my family had influence. We have all looked to our extended families and friends and how they are similar and how they were different to our own immediate family life. I feel like I took the best of what I could from prior generations, from my siblings and friends to create the best *me* I could be.

As I ponder my career journey, I have come to believe that life is not so much about what we do. I have come to believe that life is so much more about who we are and what we think. Our mindset—how we think—makes all the difference. Once we achieve a positive state of mind—when we focus on abundance—we can accomplish anything. On the contrary, when our mindset is negative and not focused on abundance, it is likely that nothing positive will be accomplished.

Choose to think positively and to focus on abundance in your life.

If you took a snapshot of my life today, you would see that I own two businesses. My business coaching firm supports the growth of businesses in the North Carolina Triad by showing owners and corporate leaders how to gain more time, improve company teams and collaborations and to add more money on their "bottom-line." In addition, I do a bit of public speaking on business success and sit on the board of a few companies as well. That is the business side of what I do.

I also focus on a different kind of growth. My family and I own a Black Perigord truffle orchard and small farm. We are working to get the orchard and farm to a place that will provide additional income well into our retirement. I like the phrase that a colleague of mine coined regarding the venture—*planting for your retirement*. I have expanded my mindset of abundance to *plant* for retirement and in doing so have increased the possibilities for the future.

How did I get here? To sum it up, I got here through example from my family, the counsel that I've received from a few smart mentors and the counsel that I've received from that *little voice in my head*. It was *in my head*—in my subconscious—that I took cues from my environment to form the *me* that I have become. It was from my education, my family, my faith, my victories and all too often from my mistakes that I have become the person I am today. I credit that *voice in my head* and how I have been able to interpret that *voice* for my achievements.

There have been times in my life when I've thought, How can I be so lucky to have this career or this family or these friends? And alternately, there have been times when I've thought, How could I be so low? I hate my job; my life seems destined for emptiness. In reality, everyone has ups and downs. And our thoughts are really driven by that *little voice* in our head. OK, you can admit it; you have conversations with yourself all the time! I know that I do!

I used to think I was crazy—I was talking to myself silently and slowly making myself mad. Not angry mad, but a crazy, anxious, depressed kind of mad. And I thought that I was the only one who did this. Since then, I've spoken, counseled and shared a glass of wine with friends who have all admitted that that *voice in their head*, when they let *it* get control, can ruin a situation. So do not let that *little voice in your head* tell you lies; feed *the voice* positive dialogue and your life will take a positive turn!

I can recall, after my first promotion to National Account Manager back in my twenties ... I was driving down Route 95 in New Jersey, on my way to the airport for my first business trip. The *little voice in my head* was saying, "You are so lucky! You get paid for doing this!" That voice in my head drove me forward and made me work harder and harder to improve my career. I can remember that day as a pivotal point where I knew I wanted a career. I promised myself that I would work as hard as necessary to have the opportunity to do something rewarding and fun and something that paid well so that I could provide for my family.

I could go back to the beginning of my career and tell you all the little things that got me to where I am today, but I think I'll just share with you what works now. Think of these lessons as a cheat sheet to feeling happy and at peace. I'm skipping to today—to now—because I think that up until I turned forty, I probably let *life drive me* more than *me* driving where I wanted my life to go.

It wasn't until around forty, that my confidence allowed me to talk about my failings. If I could give some advice to my twenty-something self, it would be to admit and then celebrate your failings. Failures are what turn us around and make us take different and better paths.

I used to panic when everyone was discussing where they went to college and I would hope that no one would ask me where I went. Every time the topic came up my *little voice* said, "You are a failure." I never lied, but often I would change the subject. I thought of myself as less of a person because I didn't have that *piece of paper*—that college degree.

Once I admitted to myself my feeling of failure, I put a plan in place to go back to school. I met with my then CEO and told him my plans. He actually didn't know that I didn't have a degree. I thought he'd be upset, but he was really impressed with my honesty, my decision and my ability to run my department with just a high school education. I am grateful for a great high school education.

Now, for the first time in my life I was planning my life and not letting life hand me what was next. My boss even promised me a promotion upon my graduation. So in my mid-forties, I finally had the confidence to admit in public, at dinner parties and even at work events that I never went to college. You never know what life has in store but the thing that makes me happy is working toward something. It's not so much in the *having* as it is in the *doing* that brings the most joy.

It's a good thing I got control of my confidence because life from that point until my early fifties dealt lots of blows that could have and sometimes did knock me completely off the path I had set out to take. Going to school, while balancing a family and a full-time executive position, was not easy. I would frequently be researching and writing papers in airports, in hotel rooms and in the middle of the night, knowing I had to be up at 5:00 a.m. to travel to a meeting.

One evening, in the middle of my studies, I got a call that my dad, then in his nineties fell down the stairs. I had to get home immediately. Dad held on till I got there, but his neck was broken. My entire family was with him when we said, "Goodbye." Dad's death brought such a profound sadness to me. A sadness that was hard to overcome. Then a few days after dad's funeral, my older brother, Clem, called to tell me that he had been diagnosed with a rare form of cancer and that his prognosis was not good.

To say Clem was an amazing human being is an understatement. He was always such a role model to me. Clem's handling of his diagnosis taught us all about the importance of fighting for what is important. He was such an inspiration to everyone and knowing I could lose him seemed too hard to bear. Just when I could have felt sorry for myself, I got a call from my best friend and her husband. Jerry was also diagnosed with cancer and it was clear that although I had lots on my plate, I needed to be there for my friend, my brother, my family and even for myself. I wanted to continue my education and finish what I started as well. That *voice in my head* just kept telling me to keep going.

Anyway, when we said goodbye to Jerry, my brother was still fighting the fight and I graduated. My *little voice* was telling me, "You have security now; you never have to worry about your career because you have a degree! You can get through all that life throws at you." It is amazing looking back now on how insignificant that piece of paper was in the shadow of the joys and sorrows of life to come.

Planning is critical, but being flexible so you can adjust to what life throws at you and get on the path to your plan is really important. Little did I know that the year I graduated, my company would have a change in management. Not only did my career look less certain, I was starting to think that I might need to consider some different career paths.

My husband and I had recently bought a small farm in the mountains so we could spend quality weekend time with our family. We had also decided to turn the farm into future retirement income generating property. I was focusing a bit on that, when my eldest son, who was a senior in high school, came home from school to tell us that his girlfriend was pregnant! That *little voice in my head* took over and started questioning my parenting ability and the crazy worry about the new path my son's life would take, often overwhelmed me.

At the same time, my mom, now in her nineties was failing. My mom fell and we almost lost her. Mom recovered but the fall coupled with watching her son get sicker from his cancer took its toll. My eldest brother passed away when I was in my twenties and I wasn't sure my mom could handle losing a second son. Not all of my siblings agreed with the best way to handle mom. Family turmoil surrounding my mother and her care added extra stress to an already trying time in my life.

In 2007, my grandson Blake was born on Christmas morning. The last conversation I had with my brother Clem that day was to tell him about my grandson and how much that little man meant to me. Clem passed away a few days later. Mom hung on until 2010.

Everything happens for a purpose. My last day of work was on a Friday and that weekend my mom fell ill at her assisted living home and was moved to the hospital. For the first time in my life, I had nothing holding me back from doing exactly what I wanted. I wanted to be at her bedside and I was able to be there with her until the day she died.

After mom passed, I knew that the drama of the past five plus years was behind me. It was time to work with my husband to plan the rest of our life. We looked at lots of options, from getting another job, to starting a business. We opted for the opportunity to start a business of our own. I recall during the last few years of my career, siting at my desk and thinking about the possibility of someday owning a business. The thought was both exciting and scary. Now, I was actually doing it!

Just as our new business was getting off the ground, another brother, Jim was diagnosed with cancer. Hearing this news doesn't make it any easier, even when you know what is to come. The lesson is that every tragedy brings lessons and points of light. Now when I look back on those times, it is the strength of family that I recall, not the sadness.

Today my career focus is primarily on growing my coaching firm. I believe this is where I can make a difference in the lives of more people. I never thought about being a teacher or an educator, but that is what I do. I believe that business owners and people in general are too much like I was in my early years, taking what life has and not planning what they want their life to be. All I can ask is that I have the strength and focus to help them open up and find a new way of their own.

Each and every day of my life has played a role in getting me to where I am now, but the purposeful direction I began to take in my fifties has been profound in the way that it fulfills me. Knowing that I can bring peace to the leaders of businesses who question their direction and their ability not only makes a difference for that business leader, but it improves the lives of their staff and their community as well.

Life still throws challenges at me every day and sometimes threatens to throw me off course, but the trick is to use *the voice in my head* to force positive messages. I am still amazed that I can train my mind to accept the abundance that life has in store for me. You can train your mind to respond to positive messages and to accept abundance as well!

I am a teacher, sharing the message of abundance through the importance of dreaming, goal setting, planning and most importantly taking action. I hope that my legacy will center on living a life of peace, the importance of remaining positive, dreaming and then going for it.

Mary Ann's Five Inspired Lessons

- **Lesson #1**: Observe—Take in your surroundings, look back at your ancestors and watch your family and your friends. Re-connect with those who have drifted away and take from them the best of what you see. Learn from your observations and let them inspire your "Being."
- **Lesson #2**: Remain Positive—Positive thoughts drive your success. Achieving success starts with thinking it!
- **Lesson #3**: It's OK to Fail—Accept and then celebrate your failures.
- **Lesson #4**: Enjoy the Journey—It's not so much in the *having* as it is in the *doing* that brings the most joy.
- **Lesson #5**: Be Grateful and Say "Thank You"—Appreciate what you have and those who take an interest in you. And let them know!

Dedication

I dedicate this chapter to my husband Kurt who has stuck by me and loved me through all of my often crazy ideas and new ventures; to my sons Ken and Jack for the joy that they bring me by just being who they are; to my brother Joe for his example of business success and more importantly for living pop's mantra *family comes first*. To my sister—may she someday come back; to my sisters-in-law for setting such diverse examples of love and parenting; to my nieces and nephews for their unconditional love. And last, to my parents and brothers in Heaven who I am sure are praying for me every day.

Serendipity Coaching & Consulting, Inc.

MaryAnnHauser@coachhauser.com
www.CoachMaryAnn.com
www.tubernut.com

INSPIRATION AND INTROSPECTION

Anne Sourbeer Morris, Ed.D.

Reach to the past for understanding, to innovate in the present and to inspire the future!

As we wonder about the lives of those who came before us, we consider the influence their choices may have had upon us—positive or negative. In either case, the choices were theirs and theirs alone. The choices made in the past are in the past. While we perceive the choices of the past to have somehow made our lives easier or possibly more challenging, our present choices are ours and ours alone. The choices we make today—in the present—will shape our future!

Live your hours so that your days are great!

I have often thought, there is no success without *challenge*. I guess that I could substitute the word *failure* for *challenge*, but I personally dislike using the word *failure*—there seems a negative connotation. The word *challenge*—seems more positive. We need as much positivism as we can receive as we navigate our *challenging* career-life journey. Positivism begins within.

Life is full of challenges, missteps and "land-mines" seemingly designed to knock us of course—to tell us lies. Don't listen to the lies of naysayers—to those who would discourage you from following your dreams and your passions—from doing the right thing. And ... as Mary Ann advises; dismiss the negative *voice in your head*. Create a positive *voice*—in fact, insist on it!

Visualize your journey! Map your destiny! Create your pathway!

UNEXPECTED REFLECTIONS

What insights or enlightenment have you, the reader, gained from Mary Ann's chapter?

Chapter 14

Life *Through Pat's Eyes*

Patricia McGlynn, Ph.D.

Never let anyone tell you that you are not worthy, not smart enough, too old or lack courage. Go for it! —**Patricia McGlynn, Ph.D.**

My career path has certainly taken twists and turns that I never anticipated. I grew up in a rural, dairy community in upstate New York. When I was about twelve or thirteen, I began my first attempt at gardening. I took over an unused dog kennel whose fencing kept the wildlife from consuming my vegetables. The soil was rich with organic matter from years of maple and horse chestnut leaves that had been placed in there to compost. Everything I planted in that location flourished. I was hooked. This was my first foray into the world of horticulture.

At nineteen, I moved to Albany, New York. I got a job in a garden center/nursery/landscape business. I fell in love with the owner's son and at twenty-three married into the business and family. I enjoyed every aspect of this venture. Over the next twenty years, I answered homeowner questions ranging from lawn maintenance, insect and disease control, tree and shrub selection, soil fertility and houseplant care. I worked outdoors, in greenhouses and with plants every day. We raised two daughters, who worked side by side with us every chance they had. I thought I would grow old on that property but that was not to be.

As life would have it, my marriage dissolved and I found myself looking for a new career. All I knew was horticulture. I did not want to go to work for a competitor and use my talents against my family. A door opened when I decided to go to college and get a master's degree in teaching. My intention was to teach high school agriculture and use my years of experience to help students. I took all the classes required for agriculture instruction at a New York State technical college and received my bachelor's degree at forty-five years old. These classes included electricity, welding, aquaponics and other hands-on courses for vo-ag teachers. In New York, it is necessary to have a master's degree to teach high school, so I needed to go further.

The next window opened when I earned an assistantship to Cornell University. I would have my tuition waived in exchange for being a teacher's assistant for a Global Seminar class. I was in a master's program designed for future science, math and agriculture teachers. The courses I took included: teaching methodology, curriculum development, educational psychology and social policy. The Global Seminar assistant position allowed me opportunities for international travel and collaboration with universities around the world. I guided students through joint lab projects using video conferencing and Skype. Our sessions had to be carefully orchestrated to take into effect language barriers and differences in time zones. It was exciting and fast paced. The undergrad students in this class were from all different departments on campus. This provided a setting for lively debates on global topics such as population, waste management, resource management and water quality. Agriculture and natural resource students often had opposing perspectives. International students debated the American way of thinking. Students with different religious backgrounds questioned each other's beliefs about population control. It was a thrill to watch them learn how to negotiate these issues.

Just as I was ready to search for a career as a high school agriculture teacher, my dean presented me with a second open door. He was leaving to join another university and needed someone to continue the work with the Global Seminar class. I would be a co-presenter and continue as an assistant. This role would pay for me to stay at Cornell University and complete my Ph.D. I had never considered this option. This was another unexpected twist. I totally enjoyed working with college students and imagined that my new career would take me into the world of academics. I combined my love of horticulture and my desire to teach to create my research project. I studied public school gardening across the county to identify benefits and measure whether or not the gardens met their specified goals. I co-taught the Global Seminar with the department chairs of Food Science and Natural Resources. It was an incredible experience and I learned so much from my fellow instructors.

I graduated with my Ph.D. in 2005, at forty-eight years old. I thought that this diploma would be my ticket to anywhere. The world would come knocking at my door. It was then that it seemed like every door closed. My stipend ran out, I was not eligible for a college loan after graduation, I was still going through my divorce and I had sent out application after application. I was too qualified for a high school teacher and did not have enough experience as a college professor. By day I worked in a greenhouse and by night I bartended in a local pub. Eventually, I was homeless and a friend let me stay in a room in the back of his house. I had one dog, three cats, a bed and a chair in one room. Bankruptcy was the next step on this downward spiral. I kept praying for a door to open. It was over two years before life started to shift. Finally, I was offered a research assistant position on the Cornell campus with a new bio-energy project. My time would be split between actual data collection in switch grass fields and designing the website that would highlight the progress of the research.

I thought that this position would lead to a career in the newly expanding alternative energy field. I could use my knowledge of plants and research methods to help study crops and create educational materials for the public. Another unexpected turn was about to appear. I was in the switch grass field when an old high school friend called from the California coast. He asked if I had ever been to Montana. After answering "no," he invited me to join him there for Thanksgiving. I said, "What the heck, sure." He said, "You belong in Montana. I just got back from visiting relatives there and I kept thinking of you. You love camping, horses, the outdoors and agriculture—everything there."

After that call, the strangest things kept prompting me about Montana. I saw a camper trailer at a farm show that had *Montana* written across the side of it. Then I went to a grocery store and there was an SUV with the model *Montana* stamped on it. When I got back to my office, I googled Montana and universities—up popped the Montana State University website. It was gorgeous with the snowcapped Rocky Mountains in the background. I clicked on the employment opportunities button and looked at an interesting job listing. There was no deadline or listing date—*For more information send an email to this address*—so I did. Since I had applied for so many positions in the last couple years, I had an up to date resume. I included it with my request. Within five minutes, I had a response. The regional director wrote that the applications were all being reviewed in two days. He strongly encouraged me to get a cover letter in by tomorrow. Wow.

Those days rush by in my memory. I was called for a phone interview. By the questions that the interview committee asked, I felt they must not have read my resume. I assumed they must not be really interested. The position was for an extension agent in a rural Montana town. I had never been an agent before. In New York, we called them educators. The description was for someone that had a broad agriculture background and could teach. I didn't know Montana but the rest seemed to fit. It was several weeks before I heard anything from Montana State. During that time, I was offered a position as coordinator for a new Sustainable Agriculture program at Cornell. This was exactly what I had been waiting for. I would have my name on the door in the *Ivory Tower*. I'd be working with students and use my agriculture and education degrees. I was about to accept the Cornell position when I was called to interview in Montana. Unabashedly, I will admit I really wanted to see Glacier National Park even if they did not offer me the job. Now, I had two opportunities. Both looked exciting.

I fell in love with Montana the moment I got off the plane. It was September and the air was crisp and clear. The town looked similar to the dairy community where I had grown up. People were friendly; Main Street was adorable with its little shops and the mountains were gorgeous. I interviewed early in the morning and then spent the day in the park. I was so calm since I knew I had a rewarding job waiting for me back in New York. It was a great visit, sort of like a mini-vacation. Once I returned, I heard nothing. Accepting the Cornell job and moving into my new office was exciting. I had been in my new location three days when the phone rang from Montana State. I was offered the extension job. Now what? Everything I knew was in New York, all of my friends, my family and my daughters. One had started her masters and the other was just finishing her bachelors. Two windows open? I asked for the weekend to decide.

Each time I push myself way out of my comfort zone I experience tremendous personal growth. It isn't always the easy road and it is not without its own trials. I have wonderful family and I thought I could always come home but I didn't know when I'd have another chance to be in Montana. I was beginning to think at fifty-one I might not have many more adventures. I took the Montana job.

I have been in Montana six years now. I am conducting research projects on sweet cherries, cold hardy wine grapes, apples, pears, plums and hops. I have taught over four hundred master gardeners. My phone rings all day with questions about lawns, vegetables, school gardens, weeds and anything agriculture. This career would keep me busy for as long as I want to work. But wait, there is another twist.

When I was working at the greenhouse and the pub in Ithaca, I spent my free time hiking along *Six Mile Creek*. Inspiration filled me. Stories appeared in my head. I began writing short stories that I called *Bedtime Stories for Grown Ups*. I thought they'd be great to read right before falling asleep. My Montana job allows me to be in the most beautiful portion of the country every day. The Glacier peaks surround this little town. I live in an old 1890's cabin. Since being here, I have had stories flowing into my mind once more—stories about birds, lakes, animals and people. My dream has always been to be an author. The spring of 2013, I began a new partnership with the *Montana Woman* magazine. I am a contributing author and my stories are now seen globally. I have a blog *patriciamcglynn.com* where I provide even more content about my world. My stories have messages that help provide understandings between people and a new awareness about our environment.

This is the most recent unexpected twist and turn. I have no idea where this writing might take me. I only know that each time I held onto my faith, even if at times it seemed like it would never happen, a door opened, sometimes two.

I do not know what will come after my being an author in the magazine; maybe write a novel or a collection of short stories. I am attending a writer's workshop soon for a major publisher. I can dream of several careers I'd still like to try when I grow up. I will wait to see what door opens. Door number one, door number two or door number three?

Pat's Five Inspired Lessons

- **Lesson #1**: Pray but keep your feet moving.
- **Lesson #2**: A door will eventually open, watch for it.
- **Lesson #3**: Surround yourself with eagles.
- **Lesson #4**: Find your passion.
- **Lesson #5**: It's never too late.

Dedication

I dedicate this chapter to my family. My siblings, my mother and my daughters have always supported my dreams. They have been the safety net when I have jumped into the void.

Patricia McGlynn, Ph.D., Montana State University Faculty

Montana Woman magazine Contributing Author
Patriciamcglynn.com
Mcglynn.pat@gmail.com

Inspiration and Introspection

Anne Sourbeer Morris, Ed.D.

Change may be manifested by necessity or by choice—change may be welcomed or resisted. Change generally pushes us out of our *comfort zone* and if we are accepting of change, tremendous growth may occur. While all change causes stress—positive or negative—if we are able to somehow embrace it, the pathway forged by change may lead to surprising new options and opportunities. In any case, change is perennial in our lives and in our careers. It is how we receive change—how we think about change that may make all the difference.

Change your thinking ... Change your life.

As life's generations pass, some individuals believe that their opportunities diminish, but the *Women of Unexpected Pathways* seem to be telling us quite the opposite. The women seem to be telling us that new adventures lie just around the corner on the career-life journey if we will simply persevere and not give up—if we prepare ourselves and have faith in our journey. While admittedly challenging, it is never too late to begin again. Never "grow up!" Dream and go!

This IS your time! Wherever you are, whatever age you are ... This IS your time! Believe it! Believe in YOU! Be inspired!

Author's note: Patricia's book, *Bedtime Stories for Grownups* will be published in 2015! Congratulations, Patricia!

Unexpected Reflections

What insights or enlightenment have you, the reader, gained from Patricia's chapter?

CHAPTER 15

Phenomenal? What? Who Me?!

CHRISTINE A. MOORE
told collaboratively with Anne Sourbeer Morris, Ed.D.

*"No" does not always mean never, it could mean,
"Not now."* —**Christine A. Moore**

One can say that pivotal circumstances or life moments are triggers for reflection. The death of Dr. Maya Angelou in June 2014, brought back memories of a life and mind-changing experience from my early twenties. And, if memory serves me correctly, it was during the summer of 1987, that I read an announcement that Maya Angelou was scheduled to speak in the auditorium, at the University of Miami. At the time, I didn't really know much about Dr. Angelou, or about her work, but I had nothing *better* to do that evening, and I *did* need to get out of my small studio apartment and actually *interact* with people for a change, so I went to the lecture not realizing that I would walk away forever a changed woman—A *Phenomenal Woman*!

Lesson #1: Evolve, Grow and Believe—Stay Strong.

For me becoming a phenomenal woman is an evolution ... a process of growth. I can say, that night, listening to Maya Angelou read excerpts from *Why the Caged Bird Sings* and *Phenomenal Woman* had a major impact on my life. After that, when I looked in the mirror, I started to see a completely different woman. I started to see a woman of beauty, confidence, power and poise. I started to see a woman free to choose her destiny and to sing her own song. I started to see a phenomenal woman.

A few weeks after hearing Maya Angelou speak, I was challenged by a pastor to read Psalm 139 out loud and replace the word "I" with my name. WOW, WOW, WOW! Talk about an "Aha" moment. For the first time, I realized that I and each of us are created with a purpose and a plan. I and each of us are important to God, regardless of what people may say. From that moment, I knew who I am and more importantly whose I am! ... I am fearfully and wonderfully made ... I realized that I, Christine A. Moore, am fearfully and wonderfully made. I realized that I am here for a purpose. I realized that I am unique and beautiful. From that moment, my faith was solidified and my destiny set into motion.

Jeremiah 29:11 *For I know the plans I have for you,* declares the Lord, *plans to prosper you and not to harm you, plans to give you hope and a future.*

I am both a citizen of Jamaica and of the United States. In 1976, my parents moved our family, my sister Dianne and I, from Jamaica to America. I was nine years old when we arrived in Florida, where I spent two fantastic decades of my life.

As a child, I never considered myself to be pretty and was not always accepted by my peers in the African American community, but made close and some lasting friends with many of my other school mates. During those years, I did not understand my value or look at myself as a beautiful human being. I thought of myself to be quite unassuming. During my preteen and teen years, however, I developed a passion for cooking—cooking became therapy for me—it was my escape. Thankfully, my parents, my constant advisors and supporters, gave me the freedom to develop my culinary skills by enduring many "interesting" meals without complaint or jest. They gave me the freedom just to be myself—freedom I gratefully accepted. Freedom that helped me to be the woman I am today.

From a young age, I embarked upon my life's journey "my way" yet, always my journey was grounded upon a strong work ethic, determination, faith and the perennial love of my parents and sister. Above all, my faith sustained me. I am blessed.

I have lived a life of spiritual revelation and evolution both personally and professionally. I am in awe of my journey from my home in Kingston, Jamaica to Lehigh Acres, Florida, then to Miami, Florida and from there to Champaign/Urbana, Illinois; then to Chicago, Illinois and now, Winston-Salem, North Carolina. My education and career pathways have certainly been unexpected, indirect and to the observer, quite possibly, unfocused. But with each opportunity and experience, I gained skill, knowledge, confidence and personal strength. The evolution is continual.

Lesson #2: It is "OK" to Dream Big—It is "OK" to Change Your Dreams! Keep Dreaming!

It was my high school ambition to become a chef and to one day own my own restaurant; and although, I was accepted at Florida State, close to home,

I very nearly embarked upon a journey to New England to study culinary arts at Johnson and Wales; until, that is, I landed a job at a Sheraton Hotel in Fort Myers, Florida, in a professional kitchen. My "college plans" were put on hold. I thought, what a better way to learn my trade than to receive hands-on experience and be mentored by an expert chef? I even followed the chef to Miami, Florida to work in a small French restaurant in Coral Gables. My family felt differently, but as always, allowed me to chart my own course.

Rather quickly, I realized that working in a kitchen, even under the tutorage of a master chef, was not all that I had imagined the experience to be. However, my stubborn nature got the better of me. I was not about to "go home with my tail between my legs" so I persevered for two more years.

When I finally decided that I had had enough of the culinary business, I landed a job as a "runner" for a small law firm in Miami and soon after secured another positon as a receptionist at a PR firm which represented some of the largest hotels and resorts on the east coast. Talk about gaining a new perspective on the hospitality industry. While working at the firm, I got my Associate's Degree in Hospitality Administration at Miami Dade Community College. Once I graduated, I was able to accept a position as a staff associate at the University of Miami School of Medicine, Department of Epidemiology and later studied Business and Administrative Law and Organizational and Behavioral Management at the University of Miami.

I remained at the University of Miami for ten years. Reflecting on these work and educational experiences, I now realize that I was building the framework for my current career in event planning—monitoring budgetary activities and designing and developing materials and activities for research projects, editing workbooks, newsletters and assisting in grant writing, as well as managing the department's Work Study Program.

Lesson #3: You Can Go Home—Home is Where Your Heart Leads You.

Then, on the morning of my thirtieth birthday, I had an epiphany. I woke up that morning and wondered what I was doing with my life. What difference was I making? I was suddenly drawn to "go home." Home to me is where my parents are. At the time, they lived in Danville, Illinois, so off I went. You can go home.

Initially, I took a job as an executive assistant with American Express Financial Advisors which again offered me broad experience in organizational management. Two years later, I moved to Chicago and began working at Accenture, again serving as an executive assistant with responsibilities including meeting and special event planning, editing and distributing newsletters, database management and special projects. I accepted the opportunity to serve as team leader for a social action team, which represented one hundred fifty Chicago firm employees. My skill repertoire was growing and a course was being charted, but where was I really going? I changed jobs once again, primarily working as an executive assistant at an investment management firm. I also headed back to school, earning my Bachelor's Degree in Political Science from Roosevelt University.

Then, one day, my friend Larcel McGhee called and asked, "Miss Moore, when are you going to move out of your comfort zone? It is time for you to go on to the next phase!" I thought, what next phase? ... How could my friend challenge my life journey? Move out of my comfort zone? Why? How ridiculous. But little did I know, it was a warning that change was around the corner.

It is amazing how life happens. Opportunities arise and we find ourselves presented with options. With hard work, determination and a willingness to accept challenge and to learn new skills, our options become broader ... we are recognized for our work and mentors encourage us. And so it was that I soon found myself in the position of Client Service Associate with the Institutional Consulting Group at Callan Associates, Inc. I supported senior consultants through client service, sales marketing and quantitative research. I spent nine and one half years at the firm and eventually worked my way up to Assistant Vice President. Not in my wildest dreams did I ever imagine ... yet, there I was in a position of leadership and influence.

Matthew 7:7 *Ask and it shall be given you; seek, and ye shall find; knock, and it shall be opened unto you ...*

Thinking back, I should not have been surprised at this success. I was prepared for it from a young age. I recall my father always commanding respect in a quietly powerful manner. He taught me by example, to do the same. My father also taught me to be humble and yet, to be strong—to stick to my convictions and beliefs. He taught me to work hard. He taught me to give one hundred percent even when I thought no one was watching and never to let anyone degrade me. He also taught me to take responsibility and to be accountable for my actions.

Throughout my journey thus far, I was always respectful to my co-workers, I worked hard and I heeded my father's sage advice. On the other hand, I did not fear addressing issues that needed to be addressed nor did I fear taking on more responsibility to assure that a project would be done with excellence. I was not afraid to go the "extra mile" to achieve personal or organizational goals. I was not afraid to adapt, change or to be accountable. I was not afraid to be strong in the face of adversity, even when opposed by some who preferred the status quo and resisted change.

Lesson # 4: Embrace Change and Challenges: Be Flexible ... Change is Inevitable!

Ah, yes change. Life does offer challenges to the best of us despite our most valiant efforts. And, so it was that eventually I knew in my heart that it was time for me to make another career change. I knew that I had to be true to myself and I was open to life's possibilities, again not knowing where the path would lead. I stepped out once again, in faith.

As fate would have it, my sister and parents had moved to the Triad area in North Carolina, several years earlier. After going home for a visit in 2010, the seed of an idea was planted ... an idea which ultimately led my sister and I to join forces, work through a comprehensive business plan and go into business together ... I moved to North Carolina and have never looked back! Another unexpected adjustment of my career pathway! Wow!

Today, I am the co-owner of *M&M Meetings and Event Planning*, partnering with my sister, Dianne Matthews. With the grace and goodness of

God we are building our brand. Our business was born out of the conviction that there is a more precise, efficient and productive way for all businesses to have successful and meaningful events with dedicated and experienced planners. Together, my sister and I have more than twenty years of combined experience in client services, meeting planning, logistics, strategic planning and on-site management, bred with a unique skill set to complete events with military precision. We believe all events, large or small, educational or celebratory, should align with the mission and vision of the organization. Meeting planning is not just about finding the right venue or caterer, it's a discipline which can be the marketing extension of any organization, and the third party vehicle to bring the right people together. We are connectors!

From our beginnings in 2011, our fledgling business continues to grow and expand as we collaborate with strategic partners throughout the Triad, in North Carolina. While starting a business is always challenging, we have big plans and big dreams for growth ... In faith, we wrote down and spoke our dreams into existence. We set our goals and while we have adjusted our course a few times along the way—always collaborating and adjusting our perspectives—we have faith in our vision.

Lesson #5: Stay Positive and Laugh Often.

In 2014, I continue to dream BIG and stay positive, as *M&M Meetings and Event Planning* grows. Where my unexpected journey will lead me in the future is unknown, but with faith, flexibility and a humble heart, I will continue to believe in my mission and stand strong, not forgetting to laugh at myself along the way, as I continue to learn and grow. I am a work in progress. I am a woman of faith. I am unique, and YES, I am a *Phenomenal Woman*!

Christine's Five Inspired Lessons

- **Lesson #1**: Evolve, Grow, and Believe—Stay Strong.
- **Lesson #2**: It is "OK" to Dream Big—It is "OK" to Change Your Dreams! Keep Dreaming!

- **Lesson #3**: You Can Go Home—Home is Where Your Heart Leads You.
- **Lesson #4**: Embrace Change and Challenge—Be Flexible ... Change is Inevitable!
- **Lesson #5**: Stay Positive and Laugh Often.

Dedication

To my Daddy, Herman A. Moore, thank you for not being ashamed of being "square" and disciplined. Thank you for being my Daddy and Father. You were right ... "it" really works!

Christine A. Moore, Co-owner M&M Meetings and Event Planning

Corporate Event Planning
www.mmmeetings.com
cmoore@mmmeetings.com
cmoore@puravidapromo.com

Inspiration and Introspection

Anne Sourbeer Morris, Ed.D.

Look for inspiration in life! Be inspired to become the person that you have dreamed of becoming. The power is within you!

The "aha" moments of life surprise us at the times we least expect them. Opportunities for learning and growth are everywhere! Inspiration comes in the most unexpected moments and in the most unexpected places. However, if we remain where we are ... if we don't show up for life, the moments will pass us by. Venture out ... experience the world. See and do things that you have not seen or done before. See life through a new lens. Make a change!

Today, take one step, just one in the direction of your dreams! ... Tomorrow, take another! You will arrive before you know it!

Faith has played an enormous role in the lives of many of *The Women of Unexpected Pathways*—faith in God or in a higher power. Faith has sustained these women. Faith has enabled the women to believe in themselves and in the face of great adversary—to carry on. Faith has offered strength and hope. Faith has bolstered courage and confidence. Faith has enabled the women to think and act boldly.

Have faith. Create immense visions and bold goals. Why not? If you eventually modify your plans you will still be ahead of the rest and will have gained valuable experience along the way!

UNEXPECTED REFLECTIONS

What insights or enlightenment have you, the reader, gained from Christine's chapter?

CHAPTER 16

Beyond Borders

CLARE NOVAK

This is an awesome life; when you forget that, read the previous statement. —**Clare Novak**

At the kitchen table during my junior year in high school, the conversation went something like this; since my grades were good, I would be allowed to go to college. My parents would pay for the first semester but after that I was on my own.

Further, my major was required to be a practical one so that "if you ever need to support yourself, you have something to fall back on." Degree choices for a young woman at that time were nurse, teacher or secretary. In November of 2013, forty-two years after the kitchen table conversation, I cleared customs at Dulles International Airport returning from two years' work in Pakistan on a USAID project. Before Pakistan I'd returned from Egypt, Kuwait, Ukraine and Canada. For eighteen of those forty-two years, my work was international as well as in the U.S. I had become the people I envied, the people who casually speak of places—Charsadda, Monsoura, Au Nang, Koh Ker—that no one in my home town knew existed.

The kid from the kitchen table has, so far, visited twenty countries and forty-five of the United States. What grand design made that all possible? None. Not in my wildest seventeen year old imagination did I ever envision a global career. Not even in my wildest thirty-five year old imagination did I envision a global career, although by then, a majority of states had been checked on my list and a few countries as well.

From the Kitchen Table to Benazir Bhutto Airport, Islamabad

A career path is not a path at all. Path implies a relatively straight, easy to walk direction. Career hike would be a good deal more accurate. Hiking requires effort, surmounting obstacles, changing trails, doubling back and going in circles. Hiking is sweat equity; learning to look back to see where you've been; helping lost souls and asking for help when you're lost. There is no path from Middletown, Pennsylvania to Islamabad, Pakistan. There is one glorious hike and the satisfaction of summiting a mountain.

Before setting foot on any trail, prepare. It doesn't matter that you will bring things you don't need and forget things you do; it does matter that you study, plan and prepare. The kid at the kitchen table dutifully earned a degree in secondary education by attending first a community college and then a state university. To pay for those, that kid worked two part time jobs, got a loan and won a scholarship. Student teaching was the last semester of the four-year degree and a heck of a time to discover how eminently unsuited my personality was for high school teaching. High school freshmen gave me a cold dose of reality. I was both unprepared and unwilling to manage teenage trauma and drama. My cooperating teacher, bless her, gave me an A. "I'm giving you an A because you're smart and we need smart teachers but really you're a B teacher." I'd have given me a C.

The more important preparation for my future career was the speech and debate team. Our coach Jane Elms was the first young career woman I'd met. Her drive and strength produced a great team. On the team, not only did I learn the craft of public speaking, which proved invaluable throughout my career, it fed the travel bug inside me. It was exciting to travel to exotic places like Ohio and Tennessee. It was even more so to attend the "Nationals" in Pasadena, California. To earn the photo taken of us on a cloudy day with our pant legs rolled up standing in the cold Pacific Ocean, each of us had had to qualify in a minimum of five events. Jane's rule.

In addition to public speaking, Jane taught these career lessons:

- Set high goals and meet them.
- Keep your word.
- Pack light.

Five events meant five events, no exceptions. "When we travel, each person will be allowed one and only one bag. If you bring more than one, we will leave it in the parking lot." Fortunately, I believed her. Three other girls did not and their excess bags were indeed left in the parking lot. Packing light is an invaluable skill in international travel.

Clearly unsuited to secondary education, I did not ace the interviews I got. My parents were making "get a job" noises and so I opted instead to get a master's degree, thinking to teach college. This time I coached the speech team as well as teaching multiple sections of Public Speaking to earn my way through a degree. Ever practical, I chose Wake Forest University because it offered the highest graduate assistant teaching salary.

A master's degree later proved to be necessary, not for the college teaching career I envisioned, but to qualify for international postings. Nearly all USAID related postings set a master's as a minimum requirement. In all, nine well-spent years were dedicated to becoming and being a college professor. During these nine years, everything I owned fit into a 1970 Dodge Coronet with a roof top luggage rack. This was good, as I moved every two to three years. The Dodge went from Wake Forest in North Carolina, to Alverno College in Milwaukee, Wisconsin, to the University of Kansas to Susquehanna University back in Pennsylvania. It took many more years to realize that being a nomad wasn't what I did; it is who I am.

In 1984, there was a glut of baby boomer Ph.Ds. on the market and a dearth of professorships. Universities had not yet figured out the adult learning market and the population of traditional aged students dropped. And as they do for most people, personal events played a career role. The fellow professor I met and later married was on a five year contract. After our one year together at Susquehanna, his contract was up. He landed another teaching job but I was not able to find a teaching job in the same region and so made a sideways step into business training and development.

After spending two years in a corporate job, starting a business and never getting it off the ground and taking another organizational training job, my feet were still firmly on U.S. soil. My first corporate job had me on the road nearly eighty percent of the time. The practical coping mechanism was to own two of every toiletry and personal care product and leave one packed at all times. The travel was exhausting, exciting and fattening. The salesmen and they were nearly all men then, used my visit as an excuse for a steak dinner. A client user group meeting and the following sales meeting had me fleeing to my room to nibble on a spinach salad when I could take no more rich New Orleans food. At one of our gatherings, the guys kept buying me drinks even after I told them to stop. When I left for the evening, I left four untouched scotches on the table.

That second corporate job would be my last for nearly eighteen years. On April 1, 1994, a deliberate date choice, I put up my shingle as a consultant and corporate trainer. It was the perfect fit that took long hours of work that didn't feel like work. When you are learning how to run a business from friends, it is fun. When you work with people you choose, it is fun. When you agree to volunteer for a community service project in Philadelphia you get work in Egypt.

Several years before starting the consulting business, I began volunteering with the Philadelphia/Delaware Valley American Society for Training and Development (ASTD) Chapter—now ATD, Association for Talent Development. At that time, it was a mega-chapter with over eight hundred members. At first, volunteering was committee service, then board, president-elect, president and past president but those were not the projects leading directly to Egypt.

The year Philadelphia was completing the new convention center, our community services chair was approached by PhilaPride. What could ASTD do to support the new convention center? We agreed to do pro bono training of trainers in customer service and those trainers in turn would provide pro bono customer service training to frontline service providers such as cab drivers, wait staff etc. Harriett Mishkin, the long-time community service chair reached out to me and two other volunteers. Would we be willing to help design the customer service training and design and conduct the training of trainers?

No one said no to Harriette. She's an absolute dynamo, always energetic and fun to be around. As the four of us worked on the training program, we developed a friendship. On the committee, I got to know Ray Wells. I'd seen Ray around but had not really spoken to him much before serving on the committee together. It was through volunteering and getting to know Ray that that first incredible international assignment came.

In the winter of 1996, the second year of the program Ray was involved in, I got a call. Was I available on specific dates? Yes. Did I want to go to Egypt? YES!!!!! That was the start of a long engagement on USAID projects in Egypt, first with the Ministry of Energy and Electricity and then with TelecomEgypt. I was so determined to go and so determined to see the pyramids, I went in a walking cast, having sprained my ankle only a week before leaving. My cherished photo is me on a crutch, in front of the pyramids. I had to see the pyramids as I didn't know I'd ever return. In the end, I saw them many times, sailed the Nile, visited Alexandria and swam in the Red Sea.

For five years, I was the only woman conducting training with the program. My arrival as an instructor caused quite the buzz. The women in the class, in very short order, contacted the women from the first year's class. By lunch time, the women from both years surrounded me and asked a barrage of questions. Nahed, a chemist, went to the Chief of Party's office and gave him what for. *Why was she not here last year? We want her to teach us too.* It was an amazing, crazy, rewarding roller coaster ride.

My work was to co-train a month long leadership course for rising stars within the Egyptian companies. Later, I co-developed and co-taught an extensive training of trainers. The work in Egypt led to the work in Kuwait and to the work in Pakistan. The work in Pakistan was in many ways a dream I hadn't even dreamed that came true. It was an opportunity to make a difference even though the difference was not the one I imagined before putting my feet on the ground. In Pakistan, I created the profession of training where it did not exist. The response to experience-based training was incredible and the program to sustain it successful.

No matter what anyone tells you of international work, it won't be what you experience. Those of us in the business all joke about the perception that what we do is glamorous. Using a porcelain hole in the ground for a toilet isn't glamorous. A three day sand storm, one hundred forty degree heat, no hot water and living behind a ten foot wall topped by razor wire is not glamorous. We aren't bragging when we talk about traveling to Lahore or Karachi or Multan; we're talking about a day's work.

We do what we do, not for glamor, but for the increment. In the US, we are fortunate; we have all the best toys. Therefore, the difference we can make in people's lives is comparatively smaller. Business people in the

US are well off compared to developing countries. In international development, there is the opportunity to make a big impact. In Egypt, at the concluding luncheon for a class, a young woman took my hand and put a metal ring with a pharaoh's likeness on my finger. "I don't know how I know this but I know that meeting you has changed my life forever." It was not likely anything I taught made a difference, but rather my presence as a business woman who could and did work in Egypt.

The lifetime of experience, including entering the work world when it was still a *men's club*, was excellent preparation for Pakistan. Pakistani career women were few in the government-owned distribution companies despite a law mandating "ten percent of women" employment. Even in the worst moments of international work, I would not trade the experience for anything else.

This condensed version of a long career leaves so much on the side of the path that these observations are needed to round out the story.

- Career women were eye popping role models. Nancy Leushner, Jane Elms, Karlyn Kohrs Campbell, Irmgard Hehmann, Harriette Mishkin—all modeled how to be strong, intelligent career women when the business world was still largely a *men's club*.
- Being true to your own path means having the courage to be the "*only*" in the room—the *only* woman, the *only* Caucasian, the *only* English speaker, the *only* HR wonk.
- Contentment comes from doing work that is who you *are*, not what you *do*.
- Take the toughest professors, work for the toughest bosses—in the end they will have challenged you to do more and be more. Most likely they will also give you bluntly honest feedback. It may not feel good at the time but later it will prove the most important thing you've ever heard.
- Be comfortable with your own company. You will be alone at times; be at peace with that.
- Volunteer with no expectation of return and be open to unexpected returns.

Finally, your friends will love you for who you are. My friend Linda Farley summed up my career better than anyone else: "Clare you just don't do normal very well."

Clare's Five Inspired Lessons

- **Lesson #1**: Work toward goals—then follow the good fortune coming out of left field.
- **Lesson #2**: Be a first and an only.
- **Lesson #3**: Be excited and be afraid, but do it anyway.
- **Lesson #4**: Volunteer, all sorts of gifts will come your way and you will find them in unexpected places.
- **Lesson #5**: Pack light. Baggage gets heavy fast—especially emotional baggage.

Dedication

To glorious friends and family, who cheer your journey and hug you when you come home.

Clare Novak, President

Novak and Associates
novakassoc@gmail.com
www.business-leadership-qualities.com

Inspiration and Introspection

Anne Sourbeer Morris, Ed.D.

Who knows where life will lead?
I intended to introduce the phrase *Who knows were life will lead?* at the conclusion of my own chapter—*Chapter 23*, as I also do at the conclusion of my speaking engagements. The phrase will still appear, however,

the concept is so apropos to Clare's career journey ... I must again state, *Who knows where life will lead*?

Clare's career, unexpectedly led her around the globe. And, I stand corrected! As Clare aptly describes it, life is a *hike* ... maybe even a *climb,* but since the word pathway seems more kind and gentle—we did not want to scare *you* away from living life to the fullest—from charting your own course; from venturing to parts unknown or from creating the career of your dreams ... from defining your own normal. We want you to be *prepared*, but not *scared* of the amazing journey that lies ahead of you!

Don't wish that you 'should have' ... Live!

While not all of us are *cut out* for international travel or for high school teaching, for that matter—one not better, just differing from the other—we are all *cut out* for something unique and wonderful. We are *cut out* for an exciting career journey that inspires and fulfills us ... that makes a difference in our lives, in the lives of our families or in the lives of others. We—YOU—are destined and worthy of greatness!

We all begin somewhere ... The trick is to begin! Be inspired to follow YOUR dreams and to author YOUR destiny! Who knows where life will lead YOU? Who knows what amazing things YOU will do? Ready, set, go!

UNEXPECTED REFLECTIONS

What insights or enlightenment have you, the reader, gained from Clare's chapter?

CHAPTER 17

The Universe Will Conspire to Help You When Your Purpose is Pure!

TINA KETCHIE STEARNS
told collaboratively with Anne Sourbeer Morris

Pay attention to what your heart and your gut are telling you to do, and have the courage to act on the things God has placed in your heart. Pray often, accept help and support from the people God will place in your life—(they are not there by accident!), and push fear behind you so nothing stops you from reaching your destiny. —**Tina Ketchie Stearns,** *Inventor of Go Free® Pants*

I'm just a girl with a crotch, like every other girl... I'm not special! So, how did I get to this place? I am an inventor! I am an entrepreneur! I'm just ... well, I'm just me! BUT, I did have an idea ...

While watching the Today Show one morning in 2007, shortly after Britney Spears was caught getting out of a taxi with no underwear, they featured a female doctor talking about women's health issues, head to toe. When the conversation turned to the bladder and yeast infections many women suffer from, the doctor said, "Britney had it right! Less is better for women!" Well, that statement led to a conversation with my monthly *Girls Night Out* group during which I found out that several of my friends did not wear underwear! Horrors! Not only that, several others wore thongs as a solution to panty lines. Oh, my! I wore "granny pants" at the time, so I thought my friends had all gone mad! Simply mad!

Needless to say, the thong supporters encouraged me to try a thong, and that lasted about eight seconds. I could not get "that" THING off fast enough! They told me I would get used to it, and I replied, *There is nothing about "that" THING that I want to get used to!*

Then, the no underwear supporters encouraged me to "go commando!" I tried it with my favorite pair of pants and was actually surprised at how much FUN it was to walk around with no underwear! It was great not having panty lines; it made me feel sexy—almost like I was doing something a little naughty which was a GREAT feeling! But the cross seam in traditional pants is in a very bad place—not comfortable at all, and with no underwear, it was really uncomfortable. That's when I told myself, if I'm going to go with no underwear—that cross seam has to go! That's when the idea for what became Go Free® Pants came to me. I took my favorite pair of pants to my alterations gal and had her replace the uncomfortable cross seam in the crotch area with a smooth cotton panel sewn directly into the pant, making undergarments optional. On that day, I became an inventor! Me? Yes, me!

The bottom line and the beauty of Go Free® Pants is if a woman chooses to wear an undergarment, the pant is extremely comfortable because the cross seam is gone. BUT if she chooses not to wear an undergarment, she is not only comfortable but has solved the panty line problem and will enjoy a wonderful sexy feeling that this new design provides. Let's face it; we women make sacrifices to look beautiful. My idea was to create pants that actually help a women look and feel her best. Now, with Go Free® Pants, patent-pending design, it's possible.

But, let's start from the beginning ... I believe that my idea was a God send. I believe that God has been the hand on my back pushing me all these years. I believe that God knew that; when offered the gift of this astounding idea, I would "fight like a dog on a bone" for it to be successful. God listened to my prayers for guidance and of gratitude. I am eternally grateful. God brought people into my life—people who would help make my vision a reality and they did.

Lesson #1: Pray—Thank God in advance for the people who will come along to help you and the blessings coming your way.

I also have guts and tenacity, I guess ... A "don't quit" attitude, for sure. That attitude and tenacity almost bankrupted me at one point, I must say. I do know that I was determined and would not hear the naysayers. I had a dream that I firmly believed in. I knew that I must see the dream through—because I was driven by what I am sure was a God given purpose and a goal—to establish an endowment for hospice as a result of the pants' success.

My overall career journey began over twenty years ago. After graduating from college in 1979, my first job was working as a secretary. Why? ... Because early on, I thought that was all I could do. Think back to the 1970's when job options were limited for women and the mind-set about what women could accomplish was even more limited. It seems hard to believe that that was my reality at the time. It was the reality for many women.

Eventually, "my gut" told me that there was more to life. Back to school

I went and after earning an MBA from Wake Forest University, I had a successful career in corporate travel management. I married, had a son and quit work for six years to stay home with my child. Then, in 2000, I was back in the job market, but things had changed. I had changed. I knew then that I wanted to do something different—something that would be gratifying to me and of help to others. I thought, if you were 'Oprah' and could do anything, what would it be? ... What speaks to you at a visceral level? For the answer, I turned to prayer and I truly believe that God directed my steps. I was drawn to work with the elderly. I applied to and got a job at Hospice & Palliative Care Center, in North Carolina. Ten years later ... I have never looked back. And then, the "Britney Spears" thing happened, and off I went into the world of invention and entrepreneurship; of course not knowing a thing about either. I only knew that I was focused on my goal of establishing an endowment for hospice and that I would work tirelessly to be successful. Over the years, I learned to pay attention to the signs and to the people who came into my life. To me, "your gut" is God—Trust your gut!

Lesson #2: Find your nerve—When you know in your gut you need to pursue a dream or idea, do it!

My tenacious attitude about the success of Go Free® Pants stemmed, as well, from another idea related to my job with hospice. You see, the hospice I work with is a non-profit and all hospices are largely supported by government programs like Medicare and Medicaid. The funding for those programs has recently been cut, which has put a huge added financial burden on hospice providers. In my mind, I could not let past and potentially future cuts to those programs affect access to the special care hospice provides families at the end of life. I saw the potential success of Go Free® Pants as a way for me to create an endowment for hospice to insure hospice care continues to be available to everyone who needs it, regardless of government funding. God put the idea for the pants in my heart for this purpose, and I knew that I had to do this. I firmly believe in giving back.

In fact, every time a woman purchases a pair of Go Free® Pants, she is helping a cause that is very near and dear to my heart—hospice care for patients and families facing the sad but certain reality of end of life. One thing I've learned from my years of working with hospice is that it is extremely important to be prepared for facing the last chapters of your life. Hospice plays a vital role in this preparation. So, when I had the brainstorm to turn traditional pants into a revolutionary, comfortable, sexy pant by replacing the cross seam with a smooth cotton panel and making undergarments optional, I decided, even though I knew nothing about fashion at the time, this new business could be a way to do something I have wanted to do for a long time—establish an endowment for hospice to help support the special care they offer patients and families dealing with end of life issues.

Lesson #3: Give Back—Donate a portion of your earnings to a charity you are passionate about, and reward the people who helped you when you have the resources to do so.

From that first idea, Go Free® Pants were designed and my new business was formed, but I must say, some amazing individuals entered my life just at the right moments. Yes, I definitely sought out knowledge and did my due diligence, trying to learn all that I could in this industry I had no experience in ... but there was SO much I did not know. We don't know what we don't know. I do know that without the blessing of incredible people, offering incredible connections, I could not have done it alone!

Success is not a one person show. It really does "take a village." I am so very grateful that I met Ding who helped me to create a "mock-up" to show to the manufacturer and who continues to offer spiritual support, which I can never get enough of! Then there is Chris who helped me file the patent and trademark documents to assure that I would hold the rights to my idea in the very competitive and challenging world of fashion design. Later, I was blessed to meet Bobby, my manufacturing exert and Wick, a marketing and branding expert; who continue to guide me and inspire me while we are on this unexpected adventure!

There are many more amazing individuals who guide and advise me and I am grateful for each and every one of them, far too many to name here. Can you believe one day, out of nowhere, I received a call from a representative from Amazon wanting to sell Go Free® Pants? And then Lydia Cornell, yes THE Lydia Cornell from the '70s sitcom *Too Close for Comfort*, started following me on Facebook and Twitter! Then again out of nowhere, I was invited to participate in the Pre-Oscar Week Suite at the Beverly Hills Hilton as a vendor in 2011! Go Free® Pants were included in the swag bags given to "the stars!" Can you believe it? What a whirlwind! Finally, I receive loving guidance and wisdom from my dear friend, White Star Woman, a Native American shamanic healer and spiritual teacher, who has helped sustain me through the learning times and taught me how to "follow the snake" because the road to your purpose isn't always straight. Cherish those who love and support you through thick and thin.

Lesson #4: There is no such thing as a one woman show—It takes a village, so let people help you!

I don't want you to think that my story is a *Cinderella* story. No story is without its pitfalls and mine is no exception. I had *naysayers*, both friends and family, telling me that I was crazy or that the idea would fail. I chose not to listen, holding on to my conviction. Then, at one point, in 2010, I nearly "crashed and burned" physically, I became so exhausted. In the process of maintaining my day job at hospice and creating this new venture, I forgot to take care of myself and paid a price. Also during the process of *learning*, I invested a significant amount of money in creating a website that in the end was a disaster. Lesson learned. I know now how to build a brand and a name to be successful and am so very proud of where we are now. Another hard lesson was when I invested in a partnership I thought was the best approach, but that failed within two months and ten thousand dollars later ... Moving on! I would not give up. I could not. I believed in my vision and knew my purpose was pure—establishing and endowment for hospice.

Lesson #5: Hard Lessons—Learn from your mistakes and move on ... Don't waste time with regrets for bad decisions.

And ... moving on we are! Tenacity pays. There is an incredible opportunity in the works right now—an opportunity that has the potential to assure the hospice endowment and to also address the health and welfare of a special group of heroes—men and women in the military. The first female Army Surgeon General Patricia Horoho, put together a Women's Health Taskforce addressing social, physical and health needs of women in the military. I have had the incredible opportunity to meet with many members of the military including generals who are interested in improving the health of our war fighters, both men and women. As a result, I am working on a patent-pending design for the military that will work for both men and women, as they often suffer from skin irritations and infections; and I have incorporated a special combination of technologies applied to the cotton that will help keep the war fighter healthy and battle ready.

We are currently waiting to be granted approval to test GOFREEDOM™ Pants with military personnel, as skin irritations and infections are a serious health issue for our troops. *Invention #2!* In a unisex design, no less! Patience, persistence and hard work have paid off. As of 2015, I am still working two full time jobs. Life is good. God is good. I am excited! The future awaits and the possibilities are endless!

Tina's Five Inspired Lessons

- **Lesson #1**: Pray—Thank God in advance for the people who will come along to help you and for the blessings coming your way.
- **Lesson #2**: Find your nerve—When you know in your gut you need to pursue a dream or idea, do it!

- **Lesson #3**: Give back—Donate a portion of your earnings to a charity you are passionate about, and reward the people who helped you when you have the resources to do so.
- **Lesson #4**: There is no such thing as a one woman show—It takes a village, so let people help you!
- **Lesson #5**: Hard lessons—Learn from your mistakes and move on ... Don't waste time with regrets for bad decisions.

Dedication

I dedicate this chapter to all the wonderful hospice providers who offer both the patients and families compassionate care and support during the final months of the end of life experience.

Tina Ketchie Stearns, President/Inventor, Go Free® Pants

Industry—Fashion
tina@gofreepants.com
www.gofreepants.com

Inspiration and Introspection

Anne Sourbeer Morris, Ed.D.

I continue to be amazed at the common attributes displayed by the *Women of Unexpected Pathways* —women who are primarily unknown to each other, but who have come together in this volume. The women emulate: caring, conviction, courage, creativity, determination, faith, persistence, perseverance, resilience and tenacity—I could go on.

The women appeared in my life—some were friends, some were strangers who have become colleagues and friends. The women miraculously "showed up"—many very unexpectedly! We are now in each other's lives. We are now inextricably connected—We are *The Women of Unexpected Pathways*.

All this to say, wow! Tina is one of the women I met after moving to North Carolina from Pennsylvania. Possibly, I should not single Tina out, as there have been others—like Tina—appearing magically and who have now joined my life journey—the *Law of Attraction*? I am a believer. I am eternally grateful.

Meet with open arms those who cross your path and join your journey—for a moment or for a lifetime. Give thanks for their support and positive influence in your life.

Again, I say, wow! I consider Tina a life force. After hearing Tina's story; I have no doubt in my mind that she will fulfil her dream to fund hospice. As Tina says, she will "fight like a dog on a bone" for her project to be successful. Tina has a vison, she has a plan and she has the WILL to achieve success.

I'll take *some of what* Tina has, thank you!

UNEXPECTED REFLECTIONS

What insights or enlightenment have you, the reader, gained from Tina's chapter?

Chapter 18

*An Intentional Career
and an Unexpected Life*

Marviette Usher
told collaboratively with Anne Sourbeer Morris, Ed.D.

There's greater in you and you were made for more.
—**Marviette Usher**

I have never thought of my career journey as "unexpected." In fact, quite the opposite, I have always been, even now in the midst of my desire for a career modification, very intentional and planful about my career pathway. Yet despite my solid planning and expectation of great success, my life journey offered modifications to my intentions and thrust me into unanticipated, yet important life phases.

As a young lady, I often thought about what I would like my life to look like when I grew up. I began to focus on the "greater" in us. This mindset was a result of often hearing family express that each generation should do better than the prior generation. As I grew up, I was also taught that God desires us to live an abundant life and resolved this to mean He had things in store for me to do and experience far greater than what I could presently see or imagine. Simply put "greater" means the special assignment on my life is bigger than me. The thought—*You were made for more*—has been the foundation for every phase of both my career and spiritual life's journey.

You were made for more resulted from being taught that God would do exceedingly, abundantly more than I could ask or even think. I remember that the first promotion and raise in my information technology (IT) job totally blew my mind. The raise proved to me that God had more in mind for me. After achieving several financial levels of satisfaction; "There comes a level of maturity and growth that causes you to seek for much more in life—a fulfillment that doesn't come from money," as Mr. Dwight Williams said to me many days. As a result of this maturity, I often express, I must give of myself to enrich someone else and my desire is to impact all those I'm contact with!

I have always believed that I was destined to be a successful career woman. I have always been passionate both about my primary job as a computer programmer/software developer and my love for fashion, which manifested itself in my fashion design business and also my current quest to become a National Sales Director for Mary Kay. My desire is to transition out of the IT industry to the business of fashion, faith and the impacting of lives of women.

As early as my high school years in the 1980s, I recognized that I wanted to pursue a career in computer information systems, despite the fact that the pathway was dominated by males and that I would be one of only a few women and certainly one of the very few African American women—in fact, the only Black woman in many cases. Despite this potential barrier to success, pursuing a traditional career—nursing, teaching or business—did not appeal to me.

While in high school, I observed people who did well in their careers and I wanted to do well too. Possibly, my mother's stories about growing up in a very small town and her drive and zeal to leave there determined to see what the American dream of success was all about, influenced me to achieve, yet, I never heard my mother say anything about obstacles to success, or about my inability, as a women, to pursue my dreams. The messages I heard were about my ability to make something of myself and I always knew—I had no doubt—I was going be successful. I did not accept the potential barriers to my success as prohibitive—I chose not to recognize them. I intentionally moved forward with my career plans. I took the 'buzz' phrase from the late 1990s "Girl Power" to heart!

I intentionally set my goal on my intended career and attended the Barbara Jordan Vocational High School for Careers. I did research and realized that the school would offer me the opportunity to pursue internships, connecting me to the business industry, where I was fortunate to receive vocational education at Tenneco Oil and Gas Corporation during high school which turned out to be excellent preparation for college. Again, I did not perceive that career and technical education (CTE) would be anything but an asset for me moving into the future. I was right; the CTE experience proved to be invaluable.

In many ways, even in high school I had tunnel vision when it came to pursuing my career. I did not consult with my "peers" about what they were going to do. I just knew what I was going to do. I am thankful that I was able to recognize my ability and embrace who I was and to have the courage, at a young age, to chart my course and to follow my dreams.

After high school, I was more determined than ever to break away from the traditional. So, off to college I headed, studying Computer Information Systems and earning my Bachelor of Business Administration at the University of Houston-Downtown. While in college, I realized that I not only did not wish to pursue a traditional career pathway, I did not wish to work for anyone long-term. I wanted to be my own boss, contracting my services and managing projects. Being an independent consultant would allow me to work on a variety of projects, in a variety of venues, and have the flexibility to work virtually, as necessary. Of course, initially, I had no idea how this type of career path would look. There were few work models in place and even fewer mentors to guide me. Some might call me a trailblazer and I was, but I was not out to change the world; just to live the life of my own design—a very intentional design, at that.

After college, I pursued ambitious goals and charted my course. It seemed, as I say, everything I touched "turned to gold," just as family friend and evangelist, Elester Garrett said it would when she spoke those very words into my life back in the '90s. I was achieving incredible success. I was caught up in my own world ... I was in "Marviette's groove" and nothing was going to stop me.

In 1998, my life as an independent consultant, software developer and owner of Exclusive By Design, Inc., led me to work with a corporation in Houston, Texas, for which I was contracted to work on myriad IT projects. I continue to work as an Application Developer Consultant for that corporation.

In June 2001, I added a fashion phase to Exclusive By Design, Inc. with the goal to help others define and enhance their own unique fashion statement. The company offers one-on-one consultations—reviewing style, color, fabric, etc.; custom apparel designs and clientele shopping assistance. To become better equipped to help clients, I've taken classes in the Fashion Design/Image Consultant Program at Houston Community College. At the same time, I created EBD Fortunes, LLC to now handle the software development and consulting aspect of my corporate project work.

Yes, about my personal life ... My last semester of college, I married a traveling evangelist, with no intention of ever being married to a "preacher" or becoming the "first lady" of the church. But our life's journey is not always as we anticipate. Unexpectedly in 2002, for me at least, my husband Elder Patrick Usher, accepted a positon as pastor, first in South Carolina and later in North Carolina, where we currently reside. I had not anticipated my husband becoming a pastor until we were much older and settled. My plan was to achieve my own personal goals, not to transition to the role of "first lady."

Honestly, at first I was devastated, thinking my hard work and planning would be lost. After all, I was solidly established in Houston. My solid plan seemed to be crumbling, yet life also has a way of surprising us. In the midst of my angst, my corporate manager offered me the incredible opportunity to telecommute from Houston enabling me to continue my independent consulting venture while also assuming the role of "first lady" supporting my husband and serving the church by his side. I could do it all and I still do. Through all of this, I learned perseverance.

After being such an organized planner and experiencing life not going according to my plans, my world might have collapsed without perseverance. I had to have steadfastness—a key that kept me moving forward despite difficulty or delays. I remember being taught to never change the goal/dream, but embrace changing the date. This principle has helped me in so many areas of my career that I honestly believe it's actually one of the most important principles to learn and grasp with urgency. Perseverance will develop persistence, determination and tenacity.

I am proud to have not only invested in my businesses and my family, but I have invested in the community, as well as founding several organizations including: *Phenomenal Woman, Inc.* whose core belief is that women are extraordinary, exceptional, unique, unusual and even rare and yes all have an intricate place in the plan of God. I also founded *King's Daughters*, an organization providing entrepreneurial mentorship for young leaders who are ready to embrace their greatness. Inspiration, encouragement and challenges are given to assist them in discovering their passion and purpose. Finally, I am among the founding committee of *Serve Yes Serve (SYS)*, a citywide movement of women believers united to canvass the streets to encourage and empower other women through conversation, prayer and support.

Although I love IT and thoroughly enjoy the time invested in my career, I have a very strong belief and desire to impact the lives of the women I come into contact. My ultimate desire is to see strong and independent women experience an abundantly fulfilled life and unveil any hidden talents, gifts and abilities. Women carry a lot in their hearts and minds and it affects us in all areas of our life. My organization, *Phenomenal Woman*, Inc. is the result of a sincere passion I have for women and how they see themselves even in their season of brokenness. I have been commissioned to equip women by encouraging, motivating and inspiring them to see themselves as the peculiar, unique, beautifully and wonderfully made creation of their Phenomenal God. I am very elated that I surrendered to my greater purpose and the realization that I was made for more and desire to see the same for other women!

In 2010, I became an Independent Beauty Consultant for Mary Kay building a phenomenal unit of team members in Houston, Texas; the North Carolina Triad and in South Carolina; in addition to my other endeavors. Mary Kay's philosophy of *God 1st, Family 2nd and Career 3rd* is in such alignment with what I believe is the balance to my life. Women join this wonderful organization for flexibility and more time with family; extra income potential through sales and team building; personal growth, education, training/mentorship and the opportunity to enrich other women's lives as well as purchase quality products at a great discount and so much more!

My final statements ...

As someone reads this chapter, it is my utmost intention to make sure the reader knows the investment God planted in each of us is HUGE and the ultimate goal in whatever we do is to bring Him admiration, honor and glory. We were created to walk in greatness. If you've stopped dreaming, dream again. If you've stopped moving, just begin again. Those hidden treasures in you are tied to your ultimate life purpose.

Plan your life course and live your dream so you can live the life you desire and have "choices." Live your best life now. Do it big and well. As life happens, tell yourself you can live through anything as long as you are making things better for or impacting someone else ... now embracing this idea is a true blessing. Maintain a mindset of gratefulness and gratitude thanking God for who you've become in the process.

Marviette's Five Inspired Lessons

- **Lesson #1**: Put your faith in God ... Life's phases are necessary. Embrace early God has the ultimate plan for your success.
- **Lesson #2**: Be goal oriented and take action ... Plan intentionally, but know that some goals will not be accomplished on 'your' timeline; there may be changes to your original plan.
- **Lesson #3**: Persevere: Don't permit life's unexpected events to hinder your momentum.
- **Lesson #4**: Be steadfast: Embrace who you are—recognize your gifts, talents and abilities.
- **Lesson #5**: See life as a rainbow—bright with colorful possibilities. Think BIG and have audacious faith that God can manifest anything.

Dedication

To the center of my life, my heavenly Father, for taking me on a journey that has and is continuing to manifest what He has invested in me. To my husband, Dr. Patrick L. Usher, Sr. and son, Patrick L. Usher, II for their never ending support and for being my #1 fans.

To my parents, Mr. Edward and Mrs. Marvia Jefferson and business mentor, Mr. Dwight Williams, for their prayers, support, wisdom, guidance and PUSH to live on the edge. To my spiritual mother, Mrs. Carolyn Robinson for gifting me with the book *You Were Made for More: The Life You Have, The Life God Wants You to Have* by Jim Cymbala that reminded me of my teachings during a very challenging phase of my life.

Marviette Usher, *Founder of Phenomenal Woman, Inc.*

Independent Computer Programming Consultant
Independent MaryKay Beauty Consultant
musher@thephenomenalwoman.org
musher@marykay.com exbydesign@gmail.com

Inspiration and Introspection

Anne Sourbeer Morris, Ed.D.

As I considered Marviette's story, I reflected on the importance of the relationships in life ... Marviette's relationship with her family, colleagues, friends, parishioners and above all else, her relationship with God impact her every action.

Marviette's conviction for that in which she believes not only drives her career but her life journey to exceed and to excel for herself and for others. Her belief fuels her passion for her career and beyond her career, her passion for helping others.

Our beliefs are pivotal to how we perceive the world. Of vast importance, is our capacity to believe in ourselves—in our abilities, our dreams and our goals—to believe that we are worthy of good things—of abundance in our life. We are worthy. You are worthy.

Celebrate your journey ... Your unique life journey is valued! Your journey makes a difference!

Note: Marviette tells the story of "An Undesired Transition" in the book *The Princess Behind the Tear Drops: It's All Right to Cry* by Elester J. Garrett

Unexpected Reflections

What insights or enlightenment have you, the reader, gained from Marviette's chapter?

Chapter 19

Letting Go of the Parking Meter

Melissa W. Wittner

Making no decision is a decision. Take control and make sure your decisions are the best for YOU! —**Melissa W. Wittner**

I graduated from high school in 1978. It was the era of disco, *Saturday Night Fever*, platform shoes and sequins. As a young female, we were all about having fun. Preparing for the future wasn't something I dwelled on too much. I was a very good musician, and had decided that I would pursue a music degree after high school. During my high school years, my curriculum was filled with music classes and I dropped out of every *hard* math and science course that was allowed. There wasn't one time that a teacher or counselor told me I should reconsider that move, or encourage me to spend more time outside of music.

As the youngest of five children, my parents had pretty much disconnected from my schooling as well. I cannot remember one conversation around the classes I was taking, why I was taking them or preparing for anything beyond high school. There was an unspoken message that I would attend college, as all my other siblings had, but there was no thought put around a degree. I do have to admit that when the rubber met the road on the school that I wanted to attend for music, my parents dissented. I could do anything else BUT that.

So, began my post high school journey. The first unexpected turn occurred before I started school the fall of my freshmen year. I had auditioned for and was accepted into the Penn State Marching Band as a flute and piccolo player. This meant I would be going to the "big campus" at State College, a three hour drive from home. A month before I was supposed to start school, I got very cold feet about leaving home. In discussions about this with my parents, they decided it would be "OK" for me to back down and simply attend the local community feeder campus for Penn State—Fayette Campus. The whole conversation probably took one minute. It went like this: Me: "I don't think I want to go to Main Campus." Mom: "OK." Me: "Maybe I should just go to Fayette Campus first and figure out what I want to do." Mom: "OK." That's it. I am pretty sure my story would have been different had this change not been made.

So, what I haven't mentioned up to this point was my high school sweetheart of three years. He was still in college very near to our home town and had decided we should get married when he graduated. This meant I would start school, do two years then quit. This really left me conflicted, because something deep inside of me wanted more out of life than being a housewife and having babies. I really WANTED a career, like my two sisters had—one was a teacher and one was a nurse. And although my oldest sister also had a family, it was clear she was a professional. My other sister who was the nurse, was single and had a very exciting lifestyle that fascinated me—she lived in big cities, traveled and just seemed to have a real passion for life in general. THAT was what I wanted. And I had no idea how to get there. By the way, my mother loved my boyfriend and could think of nothing better for me to do than to get married, have babies and stay in Southwestern Pennsylvania.

The next task for me was to figure out what I wanted to do now that I was enrolled at Fayette Campus. I took all the entrance exams, and not surprisingly did very poorly in the areas of math and science. I had not taken calculus or trigonometry, only algebra and geometry so I couldn't even read half of the math problems let alone understand them. I took biology and "practical" chemistry in high school for a total of two science courses. Practical meant *for dummies*.

My college counselor picked up the test results from my entrance exams and said, "Honey, you need to find a non-science major to go into. You will have a fifty percent chance of failure with these scores." Note that SHE told me this. Yes, my counselor was a female. She encouraged me to stay in "general classes" for a year and to take art history, sociology, psychology and Shakespeare. (Now there is nothing wrong with *Shakespeare*, but I didn't think that you could major in it!) I did what I was told. The fifty percent failure comment stuck with me. I would be smart and listen to her—what did I know? And part of me figured, who cared anyway? I planned to quit in two years to, you guessed it, get married and have babies.

With this attitude, you would think that I would not take my classes very seriously. However, that was not the case. I have quite a competitive nature; no matter what I do, I want to be the best. So, I studied hard the first two years. I found a great professor of Individual and Family Studies who had obtained her graduate degrees after the age of forty. She became a Ph.D. at the age of fifty. She was the best professor I had, and I began to use her as my counselor versus the one I was assigned. My professor's message to me was to continue on with my degree and forget about getting married right now. It was a tough choice, but that was the year I broke up with my boyfriend. I had to pursue this dream that she encouraged and believed I could have a professional career in counseling. Thus, a pathway was determined and set (or so one would think!)

After a year of taking various classes, working with my professor and feeling successful, I declared my major. I elected to pursue a degree in Human Development—Individual and Family Studies. I had a 4.0 GPA the first five semesters of college. Clearly, I could do this. I even got an A in my required college algebra course and actually enjoyed it! At the same time, I got a job on campus as a computer operator and fed punched cards into the *Remote Job Entry* system. (Yes, it was that long ago that we fed data in to computers via punch cards!)

I journeyed on for the next two years thinking my path was set. I went to the "Main" campus and was voted President of the IFSUSO student organization that had a membership of 900 people. I rubbed elbows with the Dean of the College of Human Development and sat on curriculum advisement committees as a student. I very much enjoyed this part of my college experience. Leading and directing the work of others seemed to come naturally. At the end of my junior year however, after doing volunteer work for many agencies I made a critical discovery. I discovered that I hated the actual job of counseling. It was such an emotional-drain that I would come home from a volunteer event depressed and anxious. I found myself disagreeing with the techniques used to counsel others, and came close to failing a practical counseling class due to my stubbornness to hold on to my own techniques. After much thought, self-doubt and objective thought, I decided counseling was not the profession for me. Now what? We start the discovery all over again.

Determined to do something different and leaning on my job experience as a computer operator, I looked into getting into computer science. At that point in my college career, I would nearly have to start over again, and it looked like three more years of school to switch majors. The required courses were all of those classes I was told to avoid. I became very discouraged and was flooded with doubt and fear. Penn State has a huge campus, so there was not really anyone I could discuss this with. I tried to reach out to my advisors, but these were people I met only long enough to have forms signed. At that point, I had not had one conversation with them about my career direction or capabilities. So, in the midst of being very confused and depressed, I decided to quit school instead.

I did not want to waste any more time doing something that I ultimately hated. I filled out the forms and went to my counselor to get them signed so that I could withdraw. Thank goodness my counselor stood me up, so I left his office with unsigned papers in hand. With nowhere to turn, I went to visit my brother to talk to someone who could perhaps sympathize with my situation and at least give me a place to get off campus for a bit. We sat on the porch swing for many hours and talked over the situation. He eventually convinced me that even though I didn't know what I wanted to do to get where I wanted to go, that quitting my degree now wasn't the right path—that I should finish this degree as quickly as possible and then find a way to ultimately recover my decision. Thanks to my brother and his solid advice, I averted what could have led to disaster for my career.

For the last two semesters, I proceeded to take math and computer science courses as electives. I worked with my original college professor to get redirected. She provided me with a research project whereby I could do the computer programming work for her statistical models rather than doing the required counseling internship. Everyone thought I was nuts. I loved to program. It was fun. And I was good at it too. Imagine that! I actually graduated a semester early because I plowed through school during the summer rather than move back home and work a summer job. Thus in March 1982, at the height of *Reaganomics*, I was a fresh college grad with a degree in Individual and Family Studies (AKA Counseling)—looking for a job. Not a pretty hiring picture, you can be sure.

After graduation, I was broke with nowhere to live. My parents were not happy with my choices in men at the time (another story for another day), thus moving back home was not an option. All I had was what I could fit into my Datsun B-210, and about two hundred dollars. This would not be the last time I found myself with a mere two hundred dollars in my pocket during my life. My oldest sister reached out to me and allowed me to move into her home with her family. In exchange for room and board, I could help with running the household. She had three very active teen age boys, and was a busy professional so she could use the help. I could use the time to look for a job and decide what to do with my career.

Thus began the job search. I searched high and low. In my major, a master's degree was required. Outside of my major, I really didn't have any training or experience that I could draw on. So, I took the best job I could find (and I had to convince them to hire me) working for McDonald's. The backup plan was to become a manager for the food chain. If I paid my dues as a line worker and did well, I could eventually apply for the program because I had a college degree.

This was a really dark time for me. I was depressed most of the time. I felt I had squandered four years of my life pursuing a meaningless degree. I had broken up with a guy I really did like, and was second guessing my decision to not be married. My parents were quite annoyed with me at the time (over other issues) and I had to live with my sister because all I had to my name was my car and the clothes on my back. I was working a job that had horrible hours and I despised. Clearly I needed to continue to find a way out of the mess I found myself in.

My sister and I started having long discussions about where I could go next. These discussions resulted in performing research in two directions, both of which I actively pursued. First, I considered and applied to become a Commissioned Officer for the Navy. This would be a way to fund my technical education without going into debt. I would need to give up four years of my life though to achieve this. Second, I found a degree program at The University of Pittsburgh in Information Science. I actually met all of the minimum requirements to be accepted. So, I applied for both opportunities.

My experience in dealing with trying to get into the Navy was not positive. I got different answers—from different recruiters—who tried to insist that I become enlisted for four years before applying to OCS (Officer Candidate School), despite the fact that they clearly say you can go directly to OCS if you have a Bachelor's of Science Degree, which I did. Because of that controversy, I decided not to go that direction. I had often wondered if the same thing would have happened to a man who had a degree with my credentials. Therefore, I made plans to start a master's degree at The University of Pittsburgh. This was a one year plan, and since I was pretty broke and didn't really want to, or could afford to live in Pittsburgh, I was motivated to finish in one year.

True to form, a month before I was ready to register for school I again got cold feet. (Remember the last time I got cold feet?) My mother was more than willing, once again, to have me move back home and live in Southwestern Pennsylvania while I looked for a husband. (As I mentioned, I was not doing so well on the men front these days.) What was different this time was that my dad would have none of that. We spent hours talking through why I was scared. I was afraid of moving to a big city, afraid of going into debt but most of all I was afraid I would fail. I was going to go into programming, into an area I was told I did not have an aptitude for, and aside from one Fortran class really had no solid experience to use to dispel that fear. My father reminded me of several things:

- Failure to try absolutely guarantees failure.
- If someone tells you that you have a fifty percent chance of failure, it means you have a fifty percent chance of success.
- When one door closes, another gets opened with bigger and better opportunities.
- Determination is a more important quality than intelligence.
- Making no decision is a decision. And it is not the best one you can make. Ever.

He offered to travel to Pittsburgh with me to get registered. We drove downtown, parked the car and put money in the parking meter. At that point, I decided to grit my teeth, hang on to the parking meter and refuse to move. (We must have been a sight in the middle of Oakland!) This was complemented by wails from my mother, "Oh Punk, don't make her do this!" (Punk was my father's nick name.) He eventually peeled me off of the parking meter, left my mother in the car and proceeded to go with me to the registrar's office. I signed up for class. I was committed. I was going.

How did it turn out then? Classes were hard, but I persevered. I took more coding courses than were required, because I was determined to get a job programming, rather than being a business analyst. It was a harder curriculum, but I had my mind made up about what I wanted to accomplish. I got used to Pittsburgh and even made some pretty good friends. I was able to complete classes in two semesters and landed a great internship that had me researching databases and writing database code. This is where I fell in love with databases in particular and this became the main focus of my career for many years. Once graduated, this same organization gave me a job, paying more money than I could have ever imagined. (When I see what college kids make now, I just laugh.) But it was the beginning of what has turned out to be a lifelong career in IT—information technology. My path has been full of twists and turns, and the journey gets more interesting between my first job and becoming a Vice President of IT for a major company. But that is another chapter for another book.

What is my message to young women who might be inspired by my career journey? There are a lot of messages that I hope you can take away with you. First, you can do and be anything you want. You only fail if you fail to try. Sometimes your family can be a positive influence, but recognize when you need to break ties and make your own way. Ensure you surround yourself with people who provide you with positive energy and feedback. Finally, never ever give up on your dream. Be inspired. Let go of that parking meter and drive down life's highway!

Melissa's Five Inspired Lessons

- **Lesson #1**: Failure to try absolutely guarantees failure.
- **Lesson #2**: If someone tells you that you have a fifty percent chance of failure, it means you have a fifty percent chance of success.
- **Lesson #3**: When one door closes, another gets opened with bigger and better opportunities.
- **Lesson #4**: Determination is a more important quality than intelligence.
- **Lesson #5**: Making no decision is a decision. And it is not the best one you can make. Ever.

Dedication

This chapter is dedicated to the family members that supported me growing up, and who continue to support me today. Sherri, Kathy, Harry, Tim; thanks for all the words of advice and love that you have provided.

Melissa W. Wittner, Vice President

Information Technology Software Services
Melissa@iwhereto.com

Inspiration and Introspection

Anne Sourbeer Morris, Ed.D.

Impact vs. Intent: The <u>intent</u> of one's words may be pure, but the <u>impact</u> of those words may be destructive.

With so many dedicated educators and counselors supporting students, I am always saddened to hear about negative experiences, yet these experiences must be shared to raise awareness of the impact of words. It is always frustrating to hear that an educator dissuaded a student from taking courses or from receiving information that would open the doors to the future. How does one know, really know how far an individual might go in life? How do we really know her or his capacity for success? Who are "we" to tell a student that she or he cannot achieve a dream? Who are we to withhold information or knowledge based upon our assumption about her or him? Agreed, we must answer questions about educational or work requirements with honesty, but we must answer in a manner which enables the student to examine the truth and make her or his own choices based on guided self-discovery.

Let us believe that Melisa's counselor had good intent. Unfortunately, the impact of the counselor's words on Melissa was that the counselor did not care enough to challenge her—to take the time to help her process and weigh her educational options and opportunities.

Inspire the future to aspire to greatness!

It is necessary to take the time to "hear" students and others as they are deciding their career or educational trajectory. It is important to listen to their dreams, plans and aspirations—to acknowledge their fears—to help them obtain training or experiences that are going to set them up for success and prepare them for the future—to empower them.

Even when you don't think you can, TRY! You may astonish yourself!

Unexpected Reflections

What insights or enlightenment have you, the reader, gained from Melissa's chapter?

Journeys in the Seventh Life Decade

The Sixties

CHAPTER 20

Starting Again

DONNA MARTIN HINKLE, ED.D.

*Start your path and keep your heart open to unexpected curves
and U-turns that may take you all the way there.*
—Donna Martin Hinkle, Ed.D.

"Donna, we don't have any money for college!" Dad announced, sounding surprised, as I was writing my salutatorian speech. The expectation had always been for me to attend college. I would go to college and be rich.

If Dad wasn't home by supper, he was drinking until the beer joints closed, and then he would come home, often threatening and sometimes throwing and hitting. Lying in bed, I prayed he would just eat the supper we left out for him and go to bed. He had finished tenth grade and mom finished eighth grade. Our house had a toilet and a water pump outside and two wood stoves inside. We rented land to farm, ate fresh vegetables from the garden all summer and canned vegetables and fruit all winter. We bought provisions from the two-room grocery store at the end of "the gravel," on credit till the crops came in, and we got cheese, butter, canned meat and other government surplus commodities every month.

I walked "the gravel" with neighbors to a one-room school with the same plumbing and heating as home. It was my favorite school! First through eighth graders carried brown paper sacks and traded lunches under the shade tree. Mom's homemade chocolate turnovers would get me oranges. The Missouri education monitor recommended against promoting me from first to third grade—I might be smart enough, but I was also the smallest kid in school.

Aunt Elizabeth bought my clothes so I could hold my head high—maybe too high. Our neighbors accused me of thinking I was a princess, wearing a different dress to school every day. In second grade, with long brown natural curls and big eyes, I was voted the Zoll School queen. Then, over our parents' objections, Missouri closed the last one-room school in the area, and I rode the bus twelve miles to Puxico for third grade. It was my favorite school!

Aunt Elizabeth bought me a used clarinet to play in the school band and a used upright so I could practice the piano lessons I took on Wednesdays with Becky. I went home with Becky every Wednesday night and rode the bus home the next day. Later, for high school activities, I stayed all night with best friends Kathy or Joyce and their families didn't seem to mind taking me in either. For "away" basketball games, I caught the bus at the end of the gravel, and got off there on the way back. I ran home in the dark. Everyone cheered for me when I got on and off the bus, and my joy outweighed my fear. When my favorite teacher asked our class if anyone was happy all the time, Becky and I were the only ones who raised our hands.

During my junior year, the high school counselor hired me as a clerk in his office one hour a day—my first paid job besides chopping and picking cotton. That summer, I stayed with Aunt Elizabeth in Memphis, so I could work full time. When she took me to the employment office, the woman said, "We have jobs, but you don't qualify." I asked, why not? "They're only for low-income youth," she said. I applied anyway. When I told Dad I needed to know our family income, he said, "But, Donna, that's for poor people!"

I was hired as a clerk at the Veterans Hospital and paid my supervisor gas money for a ride to and from work every day. Aunt Elizabeth drove me back and forth to my second job at Woolworths every evening and Saturday. Returning home at the end of the summer, I had money for my senior year expenses, including gas for the used Chevy II that Aunt Elizabeth bought me, but nothing left for college.

So I started applying for jobs instead of college. "You're too little to lift the boxes," the man at the shoe factory said, "You need to be Becky's size." "I didn't want to fall in love with my secretary," said the young telephone company executive. He offered me the job.

When my school counselor asked about my college applications, I told him I didn't have any money for college. He called the financial aid director at Southeast Missouri State, and he and my favorite teacher wrote recommendations for me. I used the last of my summer savings to pay the application fee.

It was my favorite school! My salutatorian status got me free tuition my first year, my family income got me federal grants and loans and my Aunt Elizabeth got me some clothes. I worked in the secretarial pool that first summer, where the director always frowned at me, even though I had been the best typist and stenographer at Puxico High. One day she looked down at me and said that the financial aid director wanted me to work as a clerk in his office, and I couldn't hide my relief!

I took dictation and typed and filed while earning degrees in English and sociology. The summer between my junior and senior years, I worked full time as a clerk at the Cape Girardeau city manager's office. But I still found myself without enough money to cover expenses. I told a friend I was going to drop out and work full time until I saved enough. In a few days, I received a check from her dad, who I never met. I sent him a small re-payment from my next paycheck, which he returned with a note. "Thank you, Donna, but if I needed the money, I wouldn't have given it to you."

My professors named me *Outstanding English Major* and asked me to stay as a graduate assistant, but I was ready to start a full-time career and marry an Army veteran who was using the G.I. Bill for college. Ready for a change from office work, I waited tables for two months until the Community Action Agency hired me to work with community leaders and direct their first voluntary action center.

The next year, I ran into a friend who had majored in English also. She told me about her school's job opening, which the teacher's association didn't want filled because they were protesting the termination of the previous teacher. I applied anyway. At my first teachers' association meeting, the president stood in front of the group and said they had hoped no teacher would accept the job. I made a motion that we all resign in protest. No one seconded, and I taught English and sociology for two years and earned fifteen graduate hours in English, until my husband finished college and got a job on the other side of the state.

We moved, and my husband decided to start again with the Army. He went to Ft. Leonard Wood, Ft. Huachuca and Zweibruecken, Germany, while I taught English in Bourbon, Missouri. When the school year ended, I flew to Germany, got a job teaching English to soldiers at the Army Education Center and a second job as a clerk at the recreation center. There were no English master's degree programs, so I started my Master's Degree in Counseling with Ball State University.

There were no English teacher openings, but I saw an ad for assistants, teachers and director at the preschool run by parents on post. I'd never taught children younger than middle school but maybe I could be a teacher assistant, I thought. When the parents asked me to direct the school and teach, I went to every early childhood training workshop offered. Every Friday night I collapsed on my couch, exhausted. Preschoolers don't sit down and follow instructions. It was my favorite job! I hated leaving my children and co-workers, but the Army moved us to Heidelberg, Germany to start again.

The nurse who was directing the child care centers in two on-post housing areas was moving. With one semester's experience as a preschool teacher and director, the Officers Wives Club hired me to direct the two centers, open twelve hours Monday-Thursday and sixteen hours on Friday. I took down the "no parents" sign at the door leading to the classrooms, ordered children's learning materials, worked in classrooms and taught staff that sanitation and safety weren't everything—Children have to move, play and learn.

The Army converted informal on-post child care and preschools into official Army programs, and the Heidelberg Army personnel office determined that I didn't meet the director qualifications—I was a certified high school English teacher—not a certified child care director. Some officers' wives, who I never met, thought otherwise and pulled the commanding general and his wife out of the theater in the middle of a movie to tell them so. The Army personnel office hired me as a GS-7 Army Child Care Director!

I didn't tell parents that we provided custodial, not educational, child care; but I rode the bus back and forth to take kids from full-day child care to part-day preschool education. After a year and a legal separation from my husband, I accepted the first child care and preschool coordinator job in Augsburg, Germany. The Heidelberg coordinator replaced me with two GS-7 directors, one for each center.

My new GS-9 job was in an old building with a cavernous child care room for children from six months to twelve years old on one end, individual preschool classrooms on the other end and rats in the attic. Not yet understanding the Army chain of command, I wrote a memo to the post commander about the building, and got a call from his facilities engineer about starting a renovation. I directed part-day preschool teachers to also teach in full-day child care, not without their protests, and I didn't tell parents that we provided mostly custodial, not educational, child care.

After a year, I was promoted to GS-11 to coordinate child care and preschool throughout Army VII Corps and then to a GS-12 Division Chief. It was my favorite job! I traveled throughout half of Germany, getting to know child care and preschool coordinators at every post. I wrote reports with my observations, but we didn't share them with parents.

I invited the VII Corps Commanding General to meet with and listen to child care and preschool coordinators. After the meeting, he signed the memo I wrote that ordered his post commanders to hire one teacher for each age group in their child care centers, repair their child care facilities and buy children's equipment and supplies. When he visited a VII Corps post, where the commander assembled Special Forces for a demonstration, he said, "I've seen demonstrations many times. Show me your child care center." One year later, I invited him to meet with child care and preschool coordinators again and a beaming 3-Star General said it was the first time anyone had reported back and thanked him.

After six years in Germany and a divorce, I started again, in El Paso where I could sleep on my brother's couch. The YWCA hired me to replace a child care center director who they had fired. I worked 6:00 a.m.—6:00 p.m. every day, and sat on my couch every night, grateful to listen to no one calling my name. At the end of six months, I had replaced everyone except the cook and was promoted to oversee child care centers and family child care homes throughout the city. We didn't tell parents that we provided custodial, not educational, child care.

The Army Air Defense Artillery School, in El Paso, offered me a GS-9 position to develop soldier training and tests. I started again. I took graduate courses in adult education on week-ends and worked up to GS-12 Division Chief again. Sometimes reassuring soldier and retired soldier co-workers, I said, "You're right, I've never been an Air Defense Artillery soldier. I've also never been stupid, so explain this to me and I'll catch on."

After a year with the YWCA and four years with Air Defense Artillery, Army headquarters called from Washington D.C.! Returning to child care, I led a multi-disciplinary inspection team throughout the Army. Thanks to the new Military Child Care Act, when the West Point commander argued with my team about their inspection findings, I was able to say, "Sir, fix it or close it." But, we didn't share inspection reports with parents.

When the first U.S. Child Care Office offered me a GS-13, I said, "You've made me the happiest person in the world!" I led the review of what states and tribes were doing with the new Child Care and Development Block Grant and coordinated technical assistance. And I worked all weekend every weekend, to get my Doctorate in Child and Youth Studies with Nova Southeastern University.

After representing the Child Care Office at a Department of Education meeting, I was offered a GS-14 position to oversee educational research projects. I told some nationally known scientists that they were misleading parents, educators, policymakers and the public with conclusions that were not proven by research. A university president wrote to the Secretary of Education about academic freedom. An early childhood researcher threatened to ask Congress for direct funding without middlemen, and I agreed, "You'll get to spend your time justifying education research funds and answering Congressional inquiries about how you're using the funds."

Army headquarters called again, this time with "an offer you can't refuse" to coordinate the design and opening of their largest center, with child care, preschool and school-age programs for four hundred thirty-eight children from six weeks to eighteen years old, while improving the program operating in the "old" center. We didn't tell the Pentagon and other military families that the "old" center was well-known at headquarters for custodial, not educational, child care.

I moved to North Carolina and continued to inspect and assist Army programs, while also chairing the county Smart Start Program committee and Board of Directors. Early childhood leaders continued talking with each other about inadequate standards, teacher and caregiver wages and training and learning environments. But we didn't talk openly and honestly with parents. Federal, state and local policies suggested that any legally operating program was fine.

So I started again. I founded ChildCareDecision.com to offer professional advice and hands-on help to parents who are making child care and preschool decisions, because no one else does. I talk openly and honestly about child care and preschool in non-bureaucratic and non-technical language that's easy for parents to quickly understand and use. I visit child care and preschools for parents or with them, discuss observations with them and the program directors. I give them complete information in written reports. It's my favorite job!

Donna's Five Inspired Lessons

- **Lesson #1**: Do what's necessary so that you can do what's possible.
- **Lesson #2**: Prepare.
- **Lesson #3**: Work.
- **Lesson #4**: Keep at it.
- **Lesson #5**: Appreciate every gift, every challenge and every chance to do something that makes a difference.

Dedication

To the angels who saved me from the sinkholes in my pathway. I could not be me now without you then.

Dr. Donna Martin Hinkle, Founder, Child Care Decision

Child and Youth Programs, Parenting, and Education
ChildCareDecision.com
Donna@ChildCareDecision.com

Inspiration and Introspection

Anne Sourbeer Morris, Ed.D.

Although much feared and frequently despised *change* is inescapable. Change is certain. Change is constant. We might suppose therefore that change would be predicted, expected and even welcomed, as it is our frequent companion on our career journey. We might expect that we would somehow anticipate, plan and prepare for eventual change. Yet, often we are not prepared—not in the least. Change emerges as an unexpected surprise.

To Change Your Life ... Change direction, strategy or perspective!

But what if we looked at change from a different lens as Donna did when she first headed to Germany? She viewed change as the opportunity for a great adventure! And, when her family was frequently transferred, Donna re-trained and re-tooled. She intentionally gained new knowledge and skill. Donna was flexible and her flexibility resulted in her career being catapulted to great heights—beyond her wildest dreams—with each new position becoming her "favorite job!"

Flexibility! ... Flexibility! ... Flexibility!

As a counselor helping students with career and educational development, I often thought of the attributes students might possess that could facilitate their career success. Without question, flexibility would appear on the list. Yes, if I could offer gifts to my students, the ability to be flexible would be one—the flexibility to react to change with dignity; to respond to change creatively and to discover the opportunities offered by change. We don't always have to be thrilled about change, but we may choose how we react to change.

Unexpected Reflections

What insights or enlightenment have you, the reader, gained from Donna's chapter?

Chapter 21

Becoming a Woman of Substance

Victoria N. Scott

Make your life a work of art ~ a robe of many colors!
—Victoria N. Scott

Some of you may remember the series of books *The Harte Family Saga*, written on the life of Emma Harte, by Barbara Taylor Bradford; particularly the first volume in the series *A Women of Substance*. For years Emma Harte was my role model and I quote:

> *Determined to rise above all that she has ever known, a young and impoverished Emma Harte embarks on a journey first of survival, then of unimaginable achievement. Driven to succeed, the iron-willed Emma parlays a small shop into the world's greatest department store and an international business empire:* Harte Enterprises.

Every time I would reach a plateau in my career, I would again reach for this book and Emma would be my exemplar!

My early years in rural Kansas were bleak. My father worked with a crew of men that moved with the combines across the vast Midwest harvesting wheat. During the off seasons, we moved around a lot as my father sought work. Often, our band of eight children slept on the floor of my grandparents' three room house. My transient childhood exposed me to a vastly different America than the one most of my demographic experienced. Living close to railroad tracks, it was not uncommon to have hobos stop by the house for food. An outhouse shrouded with cobwebs served as our bathroom and fodder for some of my worst nightmares. This was the place I most dreaded—even in the daylight. It was also where I learned to look both ways before entering, hoping to miss the eye of my grandfather. As strange and funny as it may seem, my refuge and place of solitude became one of the pig houses. Here, no one followed. I could create my own perfect world.

As the oldest girl, I became second mommy to the five children that were born prior to my tenth birthday. Another son was born when I was seventeen, less than two years before I left home. Helping my mother care for eight siblings in a six room house that could fit inside a single-wide trailer and still have room to spare was my first job. With no grass to mow, we sometimes raked the yard and played in the dirt. We swung from trees on a hay-filled gunny sack. We jumped from the loft of the barn and from the animal loading chutes. We climbed trees where we would sit and eat green apples until we became ill. We navigated rusted barrels in the yard and learned to ride on a twenty-six inch boy's bike. All of these adventures helped us escape the boredom and monotony of long summer days. We were almost a baseball team with no visiting teams to play.

My paternal grandfather reigned over the yard from his railroad bench under an old tree. We learned early to be wary of his six-foot bull whip used to snap us to attention or to grab a black snake by the tail and twirl it around his head until the snake's neck snapped. My paternal grandmother was in the house tending to the switchboard that connected all of the neighbors by phone. On occasion, I would be allowed to connect a call. After my grandmother passed, my mother took over the switchboard until it was phased out in 1964. The excitement and novelty of our first dial phone was eclipsed by the gift of the switchboard room as my private room. Wow, what an upgrade! Previously, all five brothers slept in one full-sized bed, my younger sisters in a juvenile bed and I had a small bed in the corner of my sisters' room. Now I had a place for magazine posters on the walls and a mirror all to myself.

Amidst this bedlam of home and family, I daydreamed about another life, heavily influenced by the elegance of Loretta Young and the sophistication of Jacqueline Kennedy. These women came to life for me in magazines or on television. I was seventeen and graduated from high school before I saw my first movie, *The Graduate,* starring Dustin Hoffman and Anne Bancroft. I was an impressionistic, naïve girl from the country who was about to broaden her horizons.

At the age of fifteen, my future was forever changed when we moved to a small town thirty miles away from my grandparents' house. We lived in a nicer home in a respectable sleeper town with a much better school system. In this environment, I received encouragement from teachers and other students. Here I could be anyone I wanted to be ... I experienced my first self-transformation. By the time I reached my senior year, I was an honor student and an officer of several school organizations. I competed and won. I had crossed the tracks.

My love of fashion developed more fully during this period. I was fortunate to have grown up in a time when glamour and style still intrigued and dazzled. I admired the clothes worn by famous women both on television and on the cover of fashion magazines. These beautiful clothes fostered my desire to learn how to sew. With the help of my maternal grandmother and my home economics teacher, I took control of my meager wardrobe. There was no magic wand but there was a needle. I observed well-dressed women at church and on television. I studied their mannerisms and I practiced even when teased or chastised for putting on airs.

My next life changing transformation happened as a result of the Vietnam War. My husband was drafted almost as we were reciting our marriage vows. Within two months of our marriage, he was in boot camp at Ft. Leonard Wood while I remained in Kansas City. A novice driver, I motored three hours to my parent's home and another five hours through the winding Ozark Mountains so we could spend a Sunday together. After boot camp, we learned he would be stationed in Germany. I flew with five hundred other young women across the ocean to join my husband. I was as frightened as Dorothy must have been as the great tornado lifted her into a whole new world. When our plane landed in Frankfort, I was the very last woman to be united with her husband. He arrived seven hours late as a result of going to the wrong airport.

My husband was on maneuvers more than he was at home. As a noncommissioned soldier and married, we had to live on the "economy" off base. I was far removed from other military wives. To occupy my time, I improved my driving skills, met local people who spoke some English and attended German classes on base.

I met a young, well-educated Danish woman. With this woman's help, I got a job at a local sewing factory. Talk about exposure to world culture! There were women from Greece, Egypt, Pakistan, indeed from all over Europe and one American ... me! This experience awakened a desire to travel and experience the local culture. My personal interactions with these women helped me to develop a clearer understanding of and compassion for the many immigrants flooding the United States today.

Upon returning to the United States and unsure of exactly when my husband would return, my focus turned to finding a job … much as it is now some forty years later. Having graduated from a vocational high school, I was quickly hired by a local credit union. This became the foundation for my long career in the financial industry. For nearly forty years, I migrated from credit unions to banks; from insurance to medical business office auditing.

I managed to develop style even while wearing the rigid look dictated by the "Dress for Success" mantra. Over time, I became more conservative and modest in my choices allowing my career to become the focal point. I had become seduced by successfully competing in the business world and commanding larger and larger paychecks. I believed my art was working with numbers and it was. Only when my position as Regional Director of Agencies ended in 2005, did I give serious thought to my love of beauty and fashion. During those high paying years, I stashed away as much as I could; but it would not be enough to sustain ten years of underemployment in conjunction with starting my own business.

I wanted a way to express my femininity; I wanted to wear stylish yet comfortable clothes; I wanted to read *InStyle*, *Vogue* and *Elle* rather than business magazines. I wanted to explore my own voice, my own style and ultimately, my own identity. I wanted to create my own brand though I could not initially define what that meant.

My first step was to buy an existing image consulting business that worked with television station news talent; next was to establish contracts with make-up, skin-care and clothing wholesalers. I approached or should I say "attacked" my new venture with the same fervor I had my previous career moves. But this venture was not like my other careers. There was no direct line to the top. With the exception of having "my look" together, my approach was all wrong. There was no large corporation behind me with a marketing department, car and travel allowance or expense reimbursement. Needless to say, I was wrong on many fronts. First, I was the marketing department; second, there was no expense reimbursement and third, I did not have a "Plan B" should the financial world I had known fall apart. Like so many other businesses during 2008 through 2010, mine fell like dominoes.

I tried so many tactics to jump start my business. I sub-let a space in a women's gym to be in direct contact with my target clients. One month later, as virtually all of the members left when gas prices went over four dollars per gallon, I began tearing down my space on an order to vacate. Eventually, I would use all of my savings investing in "my new career" and funding my living expenses.

After that experience, I utilized my home decorating skills to stage homes for local realtors. I held events for a local artist. I worked in the clothing department of a golf store. Out of practical necessity, I returned to the insurance industry as a salesperson. Unfortunately, I was not a good life insurance salesperson. My previous experience had been in management rather than sales and with a salary vs. straight commission.

I was floundering without direction. The opportunities that had literally dropped in my lap over the previous thirty years evaporated. Whatever I had then—luck, youth, testosterone, I surely had lost it. I continued with my positive thinking, reading motivational books, spending thousands of dollars on business coaching and, of course, prayer. Now I understood why my father gave up. He had broken the chains of poverty only to lose everything because of an "oil embargo." Seriously! I was struggling not to die at sixty two years of age. My mother and sister did not know what to think. If "Vicki" could not make it, who could? In a dream, my father came to me with these words: "You were the last one I expected to be in this position." I knew these were not words of judgment rather ones of spiritual encouragement. I used the combined belief of my family to keep my embers burning.

I would like to say I got a break; but seemingly there was not one in the cards for me. Eventually, a friend and previous employer asked me to return to his office to help him to recruit independent life insurance agents. I've chuckled to myself on many occasions, my job—yes, I did accept it—was identical to my previous one from 1996—2005 recruiting and training insurance agents. But a major change had occurred in five short years—circa 2012—there were no salary; no car; no expense account; no benefits and no need for frequent flyer miles. Welcome to the new world!

Again I would love to say that I embraced this opportunity as the beginning of my lifestyle revival ... but I do not want to paint a rosy picture in an effort to be positive. This new job was not the same. The spirit of romance I previously found in my work was lost in this new reality. I no longer felt the camaraderie, the joy, the team enthusiasm that I had experienced in the past. Less than six months later, my friend and boss resigned which left our agency without direction. I followed soon after knowing that recruiting in the life insurance industry is entirely different than recruiting for the health insurance industry and the learning curve was too steep to sustain a commission-only environment.

So where does this leave my passion for fashion and helping people find their inner self? It is very much alive and well. I am finding new and different ways to promote my skills and passions without expecting it to provide the standard of living that I had known and loved. I treasure the freedom and flexibility to do what I want to do and be who I want to be. I have gained something from my free fall: self-actualization. I have discovered a new type of power and prestige—an inner strength that comes from within rather than from position, title or salary. I love my small apartment ... it is so European! It is functional, peaceful, elegant and most of all "home." Do I own it? Not this one, but I will soon be in my very own townhome ~ maybe not a palace but certainly part of my kingdom to come!

Interestingly, in some areas of my life, my old standby mantra *where there is a will ~ there is a way* ~ still holds true. I still manage to travel, to experience other cultures in person and through delightful cuisine. I even managed to return to Paris after nearly forty years. I found something far more powerful than position and money—my experiences with friends and family.

Finally, the irony of my standard of living paralleling that of my mother is not wasted. She, too, lives in a small apartment having given up her home to help one of my sisters. I know she wishes she had my energy, my friends and my fun. I wish she could experience that as well. I still have a lot to learn about life, love and living in peace with less, much less. I pray that *women of substance* will continue to flow through my life sharing little bits of wisdom. I hope my words will encourage you to embrace what IS even if it no longer looks like what WAS. With self-actualization, there is neither mandate nor rules of engagement beyond love, respect and peace.

Victoria's Five Inspired Lessons

- **Lesson #1**: Opportunity can be found in the most unlikely places.
- **Lesson #2**: There are many teachers among us ~ find yours.
- **Lesson #3**: Losing everything may help you to find "you."
- **Lesson #4**: Find your hidden talents.
- **Lesson #5**: Don't be afraid ~ life is calling.

Dedication

To all the women of substance who passed before me and who are yet to be uncovered.

Victoria N Scott, Owner, Victoria Scott Design

Professional Stylist
www.victoriascottdesign.com
Victoria@victorianscott.com

Inspiration and Introspection

Anne Sourbeer Morris, Ed.D.

There is great power in finding inner peace; in appreciating the situation in which we find ourselves; by being *present in the present* and by learning about ourselves while remaining true to our beliefs—at least doing our very best to do so. We are all human and human beings are imperfect.

Celebrate and accept who and where YOU are today, at this moment ... Love yourself as YOU are ... Anticipate with joy the evolution to YOUR future!

Although we may desperately wish to control our circumstances, there are times that our career/life trajectory is drastically altered by forces beyond our control—by world affairs or economic downfall, as Victoria experienced. At these times, we literally and figuratively get the wind knocked out of us. It is difficult to get back up. It is difficult to begin again. Our life is changed. It is during these times, that we must take time to catch our breath and to re-group. We must evaluate our circumstances and we must remember and hold on to our passions.

Seek inspiration in the life you are living ... Live well! Be encouraged to become the person that you have always dreamed of becoming. The power is within you!

When life knocks us down, we must take the time we need to stand up, but stand we must moving forward incrementally at first, but moving forward through the disappointment, sorrow or pain. This is not an easy task I ask. At times, the task may see impossible and the challenges insurmountable but at those times, we must believe that we are worthy and valued. We must recognize our inner power and draw upon it. We must know that we can and will survive and thrive. We must believe in ourselves and in our power.

Never, never, never give up ... The next moment may hold your victory!

UNEXPECTED REFLECTIONS

What insights or enlightenment have you, the reader, gained from Victoria's chapter?

Chapter 22

Hardware, Software; Womenware

Dana Winner

Hardware and software belong to women as much as to men, but when women own them they are more likely to create sustainable social innovations. I call that Womenware. —**Dana Winner**

I dedicated my life to be a "missionary" when I was just turning three years old. Now I am an operational bridge between the Christian and the Muslim world. A very important enabler for this *unexpected pathway* was "Hardware, Software; Womenware." It has been quite an arduous journey from the three-year old girl in Washington, D.C. to a sixty-something woman in Kuwait. All the energy for the journey can be seen in the purposeful three-year old girl that I was in 1956. I understood that Creator loved "all the children of the world" regardless of race or religion. My altruistic vision was something I practiced. Even as a child in Washington, D.C., I engaged in the Civil Rights Movement, defending the rights of Black people at church, on the school bus and in the classroom. I earned the nickname of "Dudley Do-Right" and worse names that I cannot repeat.

Despite being a very "religious" little crusader, I never saw technology as opposing religion and art, as so many people tend to do. I always saw hardware and software as *Womenware*. In fact "ars" (skills) and "arts" (wisdom works) have synergized my journey, the way that fuel powers the car to transport the driver to her destination. In the integration of social action, arts and technology, my dad was my role model. He was a civil rights advocate, church singer and one of the early commercial computer programmers. He took me to the Pentagon computer room when I was just turning nine years old. That was a Saturday. The next day we went to church, not far away from the Pentagon on Capitol Hill. There was no opposition between *Worship and Music* vs. *Programming and Reason* in my life.

For me, church and computer room were both "sanctuaries." Computer programmers were "priests" between people and machines. Singers and preachers built bridges between people and Creator. Computers, religion and music were my information management systems. At age nineteen, I was using my *Womenware*, programming in binary and octal during the weekdays, singing octal-based music in the evenings and weekends. I allowed society to pay me to use my computer *Womenware*, so that I could do my music without putting a price on it. As a pioneer in *Contemporary Christian Music* (CCM) my purpose was to build bridges between people and Creator. My tactics were to contemporize church worship style, perform inspiring concerts and record albums that brought comfort to the lone listener.

As a singer/songwriter/recording-artist and '70s pioneer of CCM, I had no choice but to be self-employed and entrepreneurial. With my ex-partner, we managed every aspect of our tiny proprietorship. I retired from CCM in 1982, after seven years on the road. However, I carried with me the skills I learned in those days on the road: storytelling, music and video recording. Those "ars" have been integrated into my "technical" career to create my *Womenware*. Increasingly over the years any division between arts and technology is less and less discernible. I use the computer to record music, edit video, draw pictures, write stories and articles, design and code knowledge and information management systems. The focus is on the information, not the tools. That is *Womenware*.

As I look back on more than forty years since I became a junior computer programmer, thanks to my dad, I may be the oldest female second generation computer programmer in the world. I guess I am one of the oldest *Digital Natives*. (Let me know if there is any woman over sixty who is a second generation computer programmer or digital native—I would love to connect and hear her story.) I never felt an urge to move "up" into management away from the technology. I love the creativity of the "hands on" work. I have always insisted on remaining "technical," while also developing as a business executive. That is a challenge, but I think it is necessary to being an effective IT (information technology) leader, to stay familiar, if not intimate with the technology. I like to keep updating my *Womenware*.

I never suffered an "imposter syndrome" as a woman engaged in IT, probably due to my father delineating the boundaries favorably for me in my early childhood. When my Dad took me to work with him in the '50s and early '60s, data processing was not a "male job." During my seminal visit to the Pentagon computer room in 1961, I saw the first IBM 7090 and learned about Rear Admiral Grace Hopper—a pioneer in the computer science field. I could see that the military officers who spoke about her greatly admired her. Hopper and other women were prominent in the early days of inventing data processing. Although male chauvinism made life difficult for them, data processing was not yet branded as a "geeky guy thing." The branding of IT as a "guy thing" didn't reach cruising speed until the '80s, which is when, coincidentally, the participation of women in the IT field dropped off.

By contrast to my dad opening the computer field for me, he perceived mechanical and electrical engineering as activities to teach my brothers, not me. I looked on with envy as my brother, two years younger, learned to solder electric wires. It was clearly not an activity for a girl. On the other hand, my dad gave me a Geniac computer kit for Christmas 1962—I was nine. I wired it together very quickly. Fortunately, no soldering was needed! The Geniac taught me the most important basic reality of how computers worked then and still do: electricity flowing through on/off switches to create zeros and ones. This clearly illustrates for me the seminal effect of early childhood delineation of gender roles and activities. It is a social Role-Based Access Control (RBAC) system that informs young minds which activities their gender is permitted to engage in.

It appears as though my male parent had the greatest impact on defining those boundaries for me. My mother was a traditional housewife who did not appear to influence my perception of my own boundaries. Mom said, "Be a reader like your dad," even while she was the one reading to me and singing with me. Mom gave me the basic skills, while Dad gave me my vision and my computer programming *license, allowance* and *permit*.

Far from suffering an imposter syndrome, I feel empowered and authorized to lead in IT, in music and in worship. While this made it possible for me to bring my *Womenware* to the IT field it also causes a problem with many male colleagues. Most of the people involved in IT today are male. Furthermore, they came into IT since the post-1970's "geeky anti-social male" branding of IT took root. That male branding of IT has been thanks to the marketing ploys of personal computer (PC) and PC software manufacturers/vendors. The consumerized culture of IT has targeted male consumers.

Young techie males think I am "bragging" when I say I started as an IT professional in 1972 and that my dad started in the '50s. They certainly do not believe that I built my first computer in 1963. They don't believe IT existed in the '70s let alone the '50s and '60s. Consequently, I do not fit their stereotype as an IT leader. They are unable to perceive that I have knowledge that can help them, because they think that computers began in the '90's with the Internet or perhaps in the '80s, with Microsoft. Anything before that is irrelevant in their minds. Making the male dominance in IT more exaggerated, since the mid—'80s the involvement of women in IT has been severely down. So today, being a woman in IT is far more challenging than it was in the '60s and '70s when making the machine work was the main criteria.

My self-confidence and my *Womenware* skills were the forces that drove my career forward. As my IT career was pushing me into executive positions, I moved for the third time to the Middle East to work with an Arab company. The most difficult challenge was to leave my beloved home on Capitol Hill in Washington, D.C., where I was the third generation of my family to live near Union Station. Nevertheless, this third move to the Middle East seems to be very sticky. I have been here almost fourteen continuous years and I am married to an Arab-Muslim man. If I return to the U.S. now, I must continue my purpose of bridge building between U.S. and Middle East, between Muslims and Christians. It is a deeply embedded mission, a *pathway* I must continue to follow.

Being in the Middle East has been the most *unexpected pathway*. When life took me to Jeddah, Saudi Arabia in 1983, I was very surprised. I had never thought of the Middle East as anything other than a place in the Bible. I lived in Jeddah for one year. When the opportunity came to go to Kuwait in 1994, I was taken completely by surprise. I was not looking for a change in my life. I was happily settled in a townhouse on Capitol Hill in Washington, D.C. and had a great job with projects at the FBI and U.S. Coast Guard. I was in Kuwait for one year working with the United Nations Development Program. When the opportunity came once again to return to the Middle East, I was finally getting the message that perhaps there was more to this "calling" than I had realized. My return to the region in 2000, was the beginning of becoming "settled" on this *unexpected pathway*. Although it was unexpected, from the moment I met my husband it felt like "home." Now, I know the truth that "home is where the heart is."

While my primary purpose for being in the Middle East is bridge building, it is all possible because my *Womenware* pays the bills. I am currently developing the information management system for the European Bank for Induced Pluripotent Stem Cells (EBiSC) and other bioinformatics systems. I conduct those projects from my home in Kuwait, with occasional trips to Europe to meet with the project team. Amongst the *unexpected pathways* during this past thirteen years, I am very happy about the implementation of the Iraq Ministry of Defense Human Resources Information System, in the midst of a violent insurgency. Right now, I am very discouraged by the continued civil disorder in Iraq. The violence has made it impossible to continue building Iraq right now. Ultimately, I am committed to do everything I can to support the fledgling democracy in Iraq whenever it becomes possible. For right now, it is difficult see that *pathway*, but I know that *unexpected pathways* do open up.

The *pathway* from CCM pioneer to sixty year-old Christian women living in Kuwait, working in the Middle East region and happily married to an Arab-Muslim man, has often been arduous. What has been particularly arduous is to work through what is "sacred" vs. what is "cultural." To know what can be abandoned without psychic damage and what is spiritually essential. To know what is a cultural preference or tradition and what is actually sacred. The "IT career" created a *pathway* for me to come to the Middle East, but it is theology and exegesis that makes it possible for me to resolve religious, cultural and psychological dilemmas.

What makes it possible for me to navigate the high risk cultural challenges of conducting knowledge, information and IT management projects in the Middle East culture is being grounded in my in-depth Christian belief system. I also benefit from having studied the Quran and Islamic cultural history. There is no separation of religion, government and commerce in the Middle East. Religion permeates all activities. The dominant socio-religious culture is patriarchal, hierarchical and authoritarian. Learning is by memorization, not by analysis. Nevertheless, this is a culture where people want to join the modern world by crossing the *digital divide*; yet, the essence of the *information culture* threatens their way of life. The threat of IT is that it embeds freedom of information, egalitarianism and democratic ways of behaving into organizational processes and into society itself. Implementing a progressive IT system is a revolutionary act. Building the *knowledge society* threatens the foundations of the modern Middle East and North African culture. *Womenware* will be a very important component of building a sustainable *knowledge society* in the Middle East. *Womenware* does not treat religion as separate from government and commerce. Everything is connected.

My *Womenware* skills are focused on information delivery systems. One way that I am building the *information society*, as well as bridge building, is to become an *Anglican "Reader"* (Lay Minister.) The Anglican Reader leads services, preaches sermons, and provides pastoral support and church leadership. I am not particularly attracted to religious ritual as I prefer an inspired, informal, contemporary approach to worship. However, I recognize that the Middle East religious culture is very formal and institutionalized, focused on official roles and authority. Therefore, in order to be more accepted as someone who can formally engage in public *inter-faith dialog* (IFD) events, I am studying to be licensed as an Anglican Reader with the Diocese of Cyprus and The Gulf and St. Paul's Church in Kuwait. However, my IFD efforts are an intrinsic part of my life. Married to an Arab-Muslim man, every day is an IFD.

As I write the final edit of this chapter, we are in the final few days of Ramadan. For the past twenty-six days we have fasted from before 3:00 am. until nearly 7:00 p.m. We pray together—he in his form, me in my form—simultaneously and with a unified spirit. As we observed this Ramadan, we were daily bombarded by frightening news of violence in Syria, Iraq, Egypt, Palestine, Israel, Ukraine and Nigeria, just to name the worst cases. Although we may lose sight of it on a daily basis, we are aware of being a bridge between Christians and Muslims, America and Kuwait. Love has cleared the stones and paved a *pathway* for us to be together. We are one small bridge of unity in a region that is being torn apart by hatred. It is often difficult to remember the spiritual purpose.

My essential focus on the spiritual purpose of all humanity and all human endeavors informs my mental attitude towards my work. While a project might appear to simply be an "IT project," under the hood it is a cultural revolution which may threaten a person's concept of who they are in relation to others and to Creator. Information supports the creation of knowledge. Like the printing press' impact on Europe, the *information society* empowers the powerless, creating social upheaval. While most people find it difficult to go through cultural changes peacefully, it is possible. However, for most people a spiritual transformation is resisted at all costs. It is just very hard work to go through transformation.

Most people and most societies resist change until crisis drives transformation. Consequently, the *change management* plan for any "IT Project" must provide serious and significant support for cultural change management. This includes recognizing when people are "hitting the wall" beyond which they are unable to evolve peacefully—at least in that moment. That is what is happening in the Middle East today. In this atmosphere of severe cultural earthquakes and eruptions, I am carving and paving a *pathway*. It is an information highway that supports the growth of the *information society* in the Middle East. I believe that one key to building the Middle East *information society* is *Womenware*. Women use technology for sustainable society building purposes, rather than because of addiction to technology. Fortunately, I am far from being alone in this challenging endeavor. There are many people following this *pathway*. However, in order to succeed, we need millions of people in the Middle East to walk *this knowledge and information pathway*. Like me, they probably will come this way by many unexpected pathways.

Dana's Five Inspired Lessons

- **Lesson #1**: *Purpose drives life and mostly operates at a non-cognitive level accessed through prayer and meditation.* The most powerful "activity" we can engage in is what most people would call "prayer." To visualize the desired outcome, to articulate it and to ask for it, leads to unexpected results.
- **Lesson #2**: *Recognize and sanctify what is sacred to you while being willing to let go of personal habits and social traditions.*
- **Lesson #3**: *Social skills and technology are not mutually exclusive opposites.* "Ars" (skills) and "arts" (wisdom works) are not opposed to each other. Arts and technology are inseparable and leverage each other. Art (value judgments) are indispensable to sustainable technological innovations.
- **Lesson #4**: *Women's accomplishments, especially in STEM, are usually discounted and often obscured*: The accomplishments of women are greatly discounted to the point of being obscured. Ada Lovelace, Rear Admiral Grace Hopper and Betty Snyder are just a few of the women who invented the Digital Information Age, but who are unknown to the general public. Like them, our contributions are usually discounted and we must be self-confident and self-motivated to overcome this discouraging lack of recognition.
- **Lesson #5**: *Give with no strings attached:* We like to think of ourselves as "givers." Unconsciously, women tend to give in order to get. Then they feel disappointed or even betrayed when they don't receive the expected return on investment (ROI.) We must be honest with ourselves regarding why we are giving and we must be honest with others regarding what ROI we expect. Genuine giving always results in receiving. Disingenuous giving does not.

Dedication

To my dad who blazed the trail, and to my mom, who told me, "Be a reader like your dad" and then opened a book and read to me.

Dana Winner, President

Knowledge and Information Management
www.dana-winner.com
www.womenware.net
dana@dana-winner.com

INSPIRATION AND INTROSPECTION

Anne Sourbeer Morris, Ed.D.

In the vast caverns of knowledge available to us, it is not possible to know all that there is to know. In fact, many of us don't know—we don't have a clue—what we don't know. In today's knowledge and data-driven world it is essential that we have the ability to *access, analyze, adapt, apply* and *create* knowledge. All individuals must do so from the very young to the very mature. Access to knowledge and the ability to interpret knowledge is life transforming. Knowledge is lifesaving. Knowledge is power.

Reach to the past for understanding, to innovate in the present and to inspire the future!

Dana's story raised awareness about the history of computer programming and the reasons for the current dearth of women in the field. While aware of the contributions of Rear Admiral Grace Hopper and other women and that STEM careers (science, technology, engineering, and mathematics) are male-dominated; I was not fully aware of why women exited STEM fields after being among the original pioneers—the power of societal messaging.

We stated before, *careers have no gender*. The reality is that our corporations, our states and our nation need a highly skilled, highly trained, competitive workforce in order for us all to prosper. We need all individuals—female and male—to receive the highest quality education and training available. We can no longer limit opportunities to select populations. We must expand opportunities to all.

Celebrate the differences in life; in living and in learning ... Be YOU, uniquely YOU and permit others to do so, too!

I am struck by Dana's authenticity. I am struck by her deep faith and conviction. Yes, I am struck by her intelligence, business savvy and entrepreneurship, but it is her authenticity—her honesty about her beliefs and about her struggles to make the world a better place; to build bridges where there are none; to live and love in the face of great adversity—to which I am most strongly drawn.

Stereotyping diminishes us all ... Authenticity empowers us all!

Again I say, I pray for world peace, born of love.

Unexpected Reflections

What insights or enlightenment have you, the reader, gained from Dana's chapter?

Chapter 23

*The Journey to Unexpected Pathways:
Fearless ... Moving on with Hope,
Courage and Informed Spontaneity*

Anne Sourbeer Morris, Ed.D.
AKA "Dr. Anne"

It's never too late to create good memories ... It's never too late to create a good life ... It's NEVER too late to begin again! —**Dr. Anne**

Do we really know the women—our colleagues, our friends, our relatives—we encounter on a daily basis? Do we know their history? Do we know their hearts? Do we make assumptions based upon our own experiences and beliefs? Or, do we simply co-exist and move through our own busy lives without knowing the richness of their stories and the lessons that they may teach us? These were some of the questions that drew me to creating *Unexpected Pathways*—a journey that has been ten years in the making and one that has certainly been unexpected.

The journey began with the words, "I have feelings for someone else." ... Words that started a spiral resulting in the collapse of a thirty-five year marriage, precisely at the end of my successful thirty-five year career as an educator. And ... I was so looking forward to retirement—to enjoy time together—you know, golf, travel, rest and relaxation! With those words, my expectations about the future were dramatically altered. My life was dramatically altered. And the trajectory of my career journey was dramatically altered. Enough said. Onward!

Lesson #1: Survive and thrive ... No! Prevail! Take whatever time YOU need ... but do not give up!

In the midst of the cyclone, ten years ago, the word "survival" was in the forefront of my mind. How could I go on? What would I do? How would I take care of myself? How would I navigate this new life? I was not sure, but I did know that I wanted, as I was taught, to proceed with as much grace and dignity as I could muster. I wanted that for myself and for my two daughters. Yes, it was an incredibly sad, devastating and disappointing time. I felt betrayed and rejected, but I would survive. No. I would: *Survive, thrive, prevail and ... never, never, never give up!* as my life mantra soon came to be. Something inside of me willed me to move forward, very slowly at times—very slowly, but forward I moved; working through the sorrow, the self-doubt and the nearly disabling fear. Fear loomed large but somehow I fought it off. Survival was paramount in my mind. Faith and the will to survive ultimately trumped fear and offered hope. I drew upon resilience born of childhood experiences. I drew upon the love of my children and their love for me. I drew strength from friends who took me under their wings, listened and spent time with me. I prayed. I prayed a lot.

What would I do? I was retiring and it would be necessary to again find work. For thirty-five years, I had known only education—working as a teacher, a school counselor, a director of school counseling and a transition coordinator for four school districts—rural, urban and suburban—in Southeastern Pennsylvania. I had a wonderful career serving youth, families, schools, communities and fellow educators; and I was also a volunteer serving my profession most notably on the Governing Board of the Pennsylvania School Counselor's Association for thirty years.

Lesson #2: Revisit your dreams … Invest in yourself … It is NEVER too late to begin again.

As I said, I knew education and in my mind, the next logical step was to teach at the collegiate level. To achieve that goal, I would need a doctorate, so … I took a risk and I embarked on *The Doctoral Journey* as my professors called it. Thinking back, the decision to get my doctorate was the fulfilment of an unrealized dream. Maybe I was simply fulfilling my destiny? Who knows? At any rate, back to school I went at the age of fifty-eight! It is never too late to begin again!

Ultimately, the rigorous doctoral curriculum and the extensive research required, proved to be extremely healing. Nightly study required of me a healthy life-style. That incredible academic exercise kept me focused and "out of trouble" for sure! In reality; there was little time for anything else but study, managing my home and my consulting work. And please know that I had a lot of fear—the challenge was one of the most difficult of my life—I just could not let the process beat me. In 2011, at age sixty-three, I earned my Doctorate in Educational Leadership from the University of

Phoenix Online. I learned much. I learned that I can do anything! I learned to step out in faith without fear. Honestly ... I sort of made up my adventure as I went along and did it my way! Let's call it informed spontaneity.

Oh, did I mention that in the midst of my doctoral work, I moved from Pennsylvania to North Carolina? I left my family, friends and business network—my support system. Why you ask? The driving factor in my decision was to be *present* in the lives of my children and grandchildren—a story to be continued in my next book, *The Legacy of Six*. Next book? Yes. It is a promise I made to myself.

There were also financial considerations surrounding the move, now that I was single. In North Carolina I had the opportunity to support the design and development of an online Masters of Education in School Counseling program at an area college—I love school counseling—it is among my passions. Teaching pre-service school counselors is a dream come true.

Now please understand—obtaining a doctorate or going back to school may not be the solution for everyone, but it was the right solution for me. There is no right or wrong way to react to great challenge, but without question investing in oneself—emotionally, socially, physically, intellectually or spiritually—will pay dividends.

Lesson #3: Stay positive. Be open to new opportunities and options. Cherish YOUR journey!

As Mike Dooley AKA *The Universe* would say, "Thoughts become things, think the good ones!" Did I tell you that I have a strong belief that things will work out? Not always the way we envision, but somehow life will work out—if work is put into life. It is not always easy to have a positive attitude, but I find that approaching life from a positive perspective, in general, has served me well. I am grateful for that perspective, although at times over the past ten years, I have faltered. When I slip away from the positive and from positive people, I am not joyous. My creativity does not flow. I find joy in life, particularly when I am able to look at the beauty and promise of life—when I look beyond the negative and work to stay positive. There are myriad options and opportunities, if we can only remain positive and open to the possibilities.

As I was working on my doctorate, I took the risk to create an LLC (Limited Liability Corporation) so that I could work as an educational consultant. The risk was rewarded when I was asked to consult at three area career and technical centers; specifically working with high school career and technical students—young women and men—pursuing non-traditional career pathways, such as women working in the electrical, welding, automotive, construction or engineering professions. At the same time, I was also asked to manage a high-priority industry partnership for the Chester County Economic Development Council in conjunction with the local Workforce Investment Board. It is amazing how things fall into place. These positons were made possible because of the work and networking I did throughout my career and my willingness to volunteer on many educationally based committees, representing my school districts and in support of the students, families and communities I served.

It is amazing how the choices we make impact our future and position us for the next chapters of our career journey. I hasten to add, that managing the industry partnership ITAG—*The Information Technology Action Group* focused upon the IT (Information Technology) field—brought more than a little anxiety and fear; as the dynamics of the position and the IT field in general were foreign to me. I learned a great deal—quickly. Fortunately, I was able to draw upon my creativity and the leadership and organizational skills that I garnered over the years to successfully navigate the steep learning curve. I was also a member of an amazing team of women who supported each other every step of the way.

My work with the career and technical students coupled with my experiences supporting and developing workforce initiatives such as *GETT: Girls Exploring Tomorrows Technology*—a workforce development activity especially designed for girls in grades 6-12 and their parents, teachers and counselors, to meet and interact with successful business women. GETT was and continues to be an opportunity for parents, girls and educators to learn the facts about how careers in technology can be fun and rewarding—personally, professionally and financially. Again, I was a part of an incredibly dedicated group of women who spearheaded the G.E.T.T. project. In 2015, GETT will celebrate fifteenth years educating students and parents.

My experience with GETT and other workforce development programs led me to develop a program called *B.I.G: Business, Industry and Girls*. B.I.G. was designed as a career and educational development initiative to prepare high school girls for the STEM (Science Technology Engineering and Mathematics) workforce and to encourage them to think BIG! During the school year, the girls visited a series of corporations to learn from and speak with women in leadership—CEOs, engineers, managers, etc. Generally, the events began with a panel of women, sharing their work/life history—how they arrived in the position in which they currently worked and moving on to discuss their careers, including topics such as work-life balance. During these sessions, the seeds of *Unexpected Pathways* were being sown.

As I observed the interaction between the corporate leaders, I noticed that the members of the panels, while working closely together in the corporate environment, were not necessarily aware of each other's career or life histories. As the women on these panels related their stories to the girls, the other women on the panels were clearly in awe of the amazing backgrounds and experiences shared. The girls were enthralled by the career/life journeys related by these corporate women and the way each came to be in their current positons. I personally noted the "unexpected" nature of many of the women's journeys. I will admit, it was exciting to hear the stories of women, it was exciting to see how motivated the girls were after listening to the stories and it was exciting to observe these women truly "meet" each other for the first time—bonds of awareness, understanding and friendship were unquestionably formed—The experience was terrific! Seeds of the future were sown.

Lesson #4: Seek to understand yourself and soar!—Keep promises to yourself and others.

Events foreshadowing our future seemingly occur throughout our life time. However, they may not be realized as lessons at the time.

Flash back: "Sourbeer, what do you want now?" The words of my high school Algebra II teacher resound in my ears to this day. I had raised my hand to ask a question. The state math and science fair winners—both male—were also enrolled in that class. They clearly did not need to ask basic questions. The other students, I surmise were afraid to ask. The teacher played to the class elite—predominately male. The teacher was male. The remark essentially ended my high school career in mathematics. I became a victim of stereotype threat—clearly girls in general and I specifically were not good in mathematics. It was the message I received. Years later, I had the epiphany that I was probably pretty good in math—after all, I had been placed in the class with the math elite! Ah, the power of a remark—intentional or unintentional.

My high school experiences, my doctoral work and my work with students pursuing nontraditional career pathways led me to question the barriers faced by individuals, specifically girls and women, who attempted to navigate non-traditional career pathways. In my case, stereotype threat impeded my academic progress, as I believed that I—a girl—did not belong in the mathematics or science field. Societal stereotyping may cause even the most capable student to feel academically inferior. The belief may negatively affect test scores and academic advancement. My doctoral research confirmed that stereotype threat based upon negative stereotypes about gender or race is alive and well today, decades later.

And then there was a conversation with my youngest daughter, who despite having had great academic and athletic success in high school and college and later, taking on significant leadership and responsibility in a rigorous internship; still expressed the fear that she was *not good enough* to get to the next level of her career—imposter syndrome! Despite evidence proving the opposite, she felt inadequate. I spoke with other women and girls. I performed research. What? How could this be? Our best and brightest individuals feeling that they are not good enough—another barrier to success.

Frankly, I recall feeling the same way and having to fight through the feelings and the fear that someone might find out that I was an "imposter." There was a time when I felt that my thoughts had no value ... that I was not worthy. Author a book? No way! I believed that others were better, smarter or more worthy of success than I—even in the face of evidence to the contrary. And there has been significant evidence, but how one feels deep inside may differ from the achievements witnessed by the world.

All of these and other experiences propelled have me on the *Journey to Unexpected Pathways*—a journey that seemingly has taken ten years, but in reality has taken a lifetime. I have learned to trust myself and my ability. As I reflect on the wonderful career I have had and the future that lies before me—as I seek to understand myself—I have come to understand that I am worthy to express my thoughts. I have learned that my thoughts have value. They always have. Open the flood gates!

The reality is that I have always been what you might call a *brainstormer*—an idea person! I love to generate ideas as many colleagues will attest—I love that sort of creative process. I think the doctoral experience took me *over the edge* to truly believing in myself or maybe it was the wisdom and maturity of decades lived. Maybe life is simply too short to worry about what others might think. I still have much to do in my life—to continue to educate and to serve—to make a difference. I continue to evolve.

In any case, now, concepts and ideas overflow—*Futures Inspired! ... The Unexpected Pathways Project ... Create Futures by Inspiring Futures ... The Legacy of Six ... The Promise of Hope ... The Grandteacher Morris Sagas ...* All ideas that I have promised myself that I would nurture and give life. First, my website—*Futures Inspired*—and now, the *Unexpected Pathways Project* have become a reality. I believe that the ideas have come from a power far greater than I. I am grateful.

The completion of *Unexpected Pathways: The Journey of Women in the Workforce* is the fulfilment of a concept born of experiences. It is a promise to *me* that I would see the journey to completion. Most importantly, the completion of this volume is the fulfilment of a promise to the women who joined me on this great adventure. All have remarkably and amazingly *shown up* in my life. I am grateful.

Lesson #5: Who knows where life will lead?

Letting go of disappointment and forgiving has been critical to my survival and success. My journey has been driven by love. My heart is again filled with joy, anticipation and hope.

My life is very different now than I had anticipated it to be ten years ago, in 2005, when the *Journey to Unexpected Pathways* began, but my life and my new career journey are rich with adventure. I continue to learn and to grow through success and challenge. Without question, my work and life experiences prepared me for my current unexpected career and life journey.

I am a connector. My colleagues have referred to me as a *broker of resources*. Knowledge sharing is among my passions. I must continue to do so. My future is full of opportunity and options. I look forward to my next great adventure. Who knows where life will lead?

Dr. Anne's Five Inspired Lessons

- **Lesson #1**: Survive and thrive ... No! Prevail! Take whatever time you need, but do not give up on yourself or your goals.
- **Lesson #2**: Revisit your dreams ... Invest in yourself ... It is NEVER too late to begin again.
- **Lesson #3**: Stay positive. Be open to new opportunities and options. Cherish YOUR journey!
- **Lesson #4**: Seek to understand yourself and soar!—Keep promises to yourself and others.
- **Lesson #5**: Who knows where life will lead?

Dedication

To my mentors ... past, present and future.

Anne Sourbeer Morris, Ed.D.

A. Morris Consulting, LLC acting as Futures Inspired
anne@futuresinspired.com
www.futuresinspired.com

Inspiration and Introspection

Anne Sourbeer Morris, Ed.D.

Fear may attempt to derail us. We must not let fear deter us from following our destiny.

Upon reflection, if I could give YOU anything, I would banish the fear of achieving your dreams of success—whatever success means to you. Your dreams are intimate reflections of you. Your success is unique to your vision. Hold on to your dreams. At the very least, remember the dreams of your past; so that they may be re-kindled, possibly modified but never dismissed.

Escape the burdens of your fear.

Fear of the unknown, fear of change, fear of failure or fear of success may prevent us from taking the first steps to building our future. As I embarked upon the *Journey to Unexpected Pathways,* I was fearful many times—even now, as I write these final sentences, there is doubt; but there is more pride—pride in myself, but more significantly, pride in the women who joined me on this journey—who shared deeply of themselves with the sincere goal that their words would make a difference in the lives of others. Our most basic motivation was to inspire another individual to move forward with courage and the hope of a better future to come—to embark upon the career and life of her or his dreams—to believe in herself or himself.

Faith crushes fear and offers hope.

It is my wish that YOU will follow your heart and your dreams ... that YOU will move forward with courage and confidence ... that YOU will never, never, never give up!

May your journey be driven by love.

Be inspired!

Today, take one step, just one in the direction of your dream. Be inspired; be open to opportunities and options. Who knows where life will lead?

UNEXPECTED REFLECTIONS

What insights or enlightenment have you, the reader, gained from Anne's chapter?

Epilogue

Endings and New Beginnings

Does the life journey drive the career journey or does the career journey drive the life? —**Anne Sourbeer Morris, Ed. D.**

True wisdom is ageless. True idealism is ageless. Idealism must not be "assigned" to the young or wisdom to the old. As we create our career/life journey we must embody both idealism and wisdom. We must maintain the enthusiasm and passion of the young while embodying the conviction and perseverance of those who have paved the way for us. Our hearts are ageless. Our dreams are ageless. The belief in our journey must be perennial and unwavering.

In living life—we honor ourselves; we honor the generations of women who have gone before us and we honor those who will follow. In living life, we create our legacy.

The **W***omen of Unexpected Pathways* did not see themselves as victims of life circumstance, nor were they dissuaded by the words of others proclaiming a certain destiny upon their lives. Each woman held strong to her convictions and forged ahead despite adversity. Each woman courageously gifted us with her story—with the goal to make a difference in the lives of others—to raise awareness, to unify and to offer inspiration—by recounting her journey and sharing lessons learned along the way.

Since completing their chapters, several women have stepped into the next life decade. Others have embarked upon new projects and have made new connections including those with fellow *Unexpected Pathways* chapter authors. Dana and Clare are collaborating on projects in the Middle East. Gabrielle and Melissa are working together to create the first girls robotics team in the Piedmont Triad of North Carolina. Mittie and I will be collaborating to support girls and women pursuing nontraditional career pathways—particularly in the construction trades.

Be open to new connections ... They may unexpectedly appear!

Finally, born of the expression of faith that many of the *Women of Unexpected Pathways* declared, I have been inspired to consider the role that faith may play in the career journey of women and how faith impacts the life pathway. In fact, very recently, a dear friend declared publically that there will be a next *Unexpected Pathways* volume and that it would focus on the career life journeys of women of faith. It would be an honor to produce that volume and others, if sufficient interest is expressed. Who knows where life will lead?

Be inspired!

This IS your time! Where ever you are, whatever age you are, whatever stage you are ... This IS your time! Believe it! Believe in YOU!

UNEXPECTED PATHWAYS STUDY GUIDE

1. How did you experience this book?

2. Which story most strongly resonated with or engaged you? In what way?

3. What common themes did you identify?

4. What common traits or characteristics did you identify in the *Women of Unexpected Pathways*?

5. Do you believe that age, ethnicity or sexual preference impacted the career/life perspective of the *Women of Unexpected Pathways*?

6. Did the age, ethnicity or sexual preference of a chapter author influence your response to her story?

7. Do you believe that your response to individual stories might differ if you were unaware of the chapter author's age, ethnicity or sexual preference?

8. Faith played a significant part in the lives of many of the chapter authors. How did you respond to discussions about the role faith played in the lives of these chapter authors?

9. Have the stories in this book changed or broadened your viewpoint?

10. How may life impact one's career pathway?

11. How may career choices impact one's life?

12. Does the life journey drive the career journey or does the career journey drive the life?

13. The career pathways of women are unexpected. Do you agree or disagree with this statement? Has your career pathway been unexpected?

14. What "aha" moment(s) did you experience while reading the stories of *The Women of Unexpected Pathways*?

15. Which *Inspired Lessons* were most meaningful to you?

16. Have you been inspired to modify your career or life trajectory or to embark upon new pathways? What is your goal? What is your plan of action?

Research Scaffolding Unexpected Pathways

Over six hundred eighty women from fifty (50) states, the District of Columbia and women who have lived/worked in twenty (20) nations responded to the *Unexpected Pathways Survey* introduced in October 2012 to scaffold the *Unexpected Pathways Project* and to confirm or refute the hypothesis that women's career journeys may be unexpected. All survey participants were self-selected, responding voluntarily to the *Unexpected Pathways Survey*.

As hypothesized, the majority of women who participated in the *Unexpected Pathways Survey* (63.99%) indicated that their career outcomes were in fact, *unexpected*. In other words, these women did not anticipate, at the beginning of their career to be where they currently find themselves in terms of their career journey. Interestingly, although the majority of the women identified their current career status as unexpected, 56.32% of the respondents also indicated that they were working in the career field in which they were originally trained.

While the participants in this survey were geographically and generationally diverse and represented myriad career clusters, the survey results were not extensive enough to definitively state that women's career pathways are unexpected in general. As the majority of seminal work on career development was focused on the career develop of men, it is the hope of the author that additional work on the career journeys of women will be undertaken by future researchers.

Additional information on the research supporting the project and the individual *Women of Unexpected Pathways* may be discovered by visiting www.futuresinspired.com

About Futures Inspired

Our mission is to facilitate the academic, career and personal development of individuals through the formation of visions, the fulfillment of dreams and the creation of legacies.

The Futures Inspired website is the host site for a dynamic collection of educationally inspired projects. As our site grows, we will include resources from myriad sources as well as information about the vibrant individuals supporting our work. Futures Inspired projects are designed, developed and produced by Dr. Anne Sourbeer Morris, educator, author and presenter.

Our goal is to inspire the future!

A. MORRIS CONSULTING, LLC acting
as FUTURES INSPIRED

Anne Sourbeer Morris, Ed.D
www.futuresinspired.com
anne@futuresinspired.com

About the Author

Anne Sourbeer Morris, Ed.D. AKA "Dr. Anne"

Dr. Anne Sourbeer Morris is the Managing Member of A. Morris Consulting, LLC acting as Futures Inspired offering educational consulting services to individuals, schools and corporate entities. Educational and workforce equity and inclusion lie at the heart of her work.

In 2005, Anne retired from the Great Valley School District, Malvern, Pennsylvania as the district's Transition Coordinator, supporting students with disabilities and their families. She was a former Director of School Counseling for Great Valley High School and the Counseling Department Chairperson at Octorara Area High School. Over a thirty-five year career in public education, she worked in rural, urban and suburban school districts as a teacher and school counselor. Always active in her community, Anne served as chairperson of the Chester County Council for the Workforce of Tomorrow and was a consultant for the Chester County Economic Development Council, managing a high priority industry partnership. Anne also served as a consultant to the Chester County Intermediate Unit working with career and technical students pursuing nontraditional career pathways.

For thirty years, Anne's primary volunteerism was with the Pennsylvania School Counselors Association (PSCA) for which she served in myriad capacities including as the organization's president and newsletter editor. Dr. Anne served on the Education Foundation Board of the National Alliance for Partnerships in Equity and the Guidance and Counseling Advisory Committee of the Association for Career and Technical Education.

In 1990, Anne was named PSCA School Counselor of the Year. In 2010, Dr. Anne was given the PSCA Honorary Lifetime Achievement award and was named a National Association of Professional Women (NAPW), Woman of the Year. In that same year, Anne moved from Pennsylvania to North Carolina. Immediately connecting with her community; she served as the first president of the Winston-Salem Local Chapter of NAPW. For two years, she was a member of the Board of Directors of The Queen's Foundation, Inc., supporting young women in North Carolina. Dr. Sourbeer Morris is currently an Associate Adjunct Professor of Education at Salem College, Winston-Salem, North Carolina. She collaborated on the design and curriculum development of the Salem College Online Masters of Education in School Counseling program. Her writing has been featured in publications including *Career World Magazine*.

Thank you to those who supported
The Journey to Unexpected Pathways ...
To those who took me under their wings and comforted me ...
To those who were not afraid of my pain ...
You are loved.

My Deepest Gratitude to
Danna Bouchey, Bryan Brunette and to
Jerry and Michlle Dorris of AuthorSupport.com
Thank You for Your Guidance and Support!
And to
Reynolda Presbyterian Church
Where I am Surrounded by Grace.

Photo Credits

- Wynne Renee Brown, MD, Lac—Winston-Salem State University photo, Garrett Garms
- Mittie Denise Cannon, Ed.D.—Robins & Morton photo, Justin Poland Photography
- Bonnie Dawn Clark—Amber Galloway
- Kaitlyn Green—Hazel Grace Photography—Deneen Knapper-Mulvaine Bryan
- Latoya Rochae' Johnson—J. Harris Photography
- Gabrielle J. Jordan—Rajah J. Jackson, R.J. Photography
- Patricia McGlynn, Ph.D.—Nicole Tavenner, Piknik Studios
- Anne Sourbeer Morris, Ed.D.—J. Harris Photography
- Marviette Usher—Hazel Grace Photography—Deneen Knapper-Mulvaine Bryan

A percentage of the sale of this volume will go to organizations supporting women's career development including the National Alliance for Partnerships in Equity (NAPE) and organizations supporting the career/life journeys of women and girls.

Made in the USA
Charleston, SC
13 May 2015